WINNING
CASINO CRAPS

Other books by the author

FICTION

Rapt in Glory
Nightmare of the Dark
Sweet Land of Liberty
Losers Weepers
Snake Eyes

NONFICTION

Playboy's Book of Games
Las Vegas, An Insider's Guide
Smart Casino Play
Play Bridge Tonight
Play Chess Tonight
Play Pinochle Tonight
Winning Poker Strategy
How to Gamble and Win

WINNING CASINO CRAPS

Edwin Silberstang

DAVID McKAY COMPANY, INC.
New York

All rights reserved under International and Pan-American
Copyright Conventions. Published in the United States by
David McKay Company, Inc., New York, and simultaneously
in Canada by Random House of Canada Limited, Toronto.
Distributed by Random House, Inc., New York.

Library of Congress Cataloging in Publication Data

Silberstang, Edwin, 1930–
  Winning casino craps.

  Includes index.
  1. Craps (Game) 2. Gambling systems.
I. Title.
GV1303.S56   795'.1   79-16808
ISBN 0-679-14650-4

C98765

MANUFACTURED IN THE UNITED STATES OF AMERICA

For Kimball and Jane Allen

Contents

Contents

WINNING
CASINO CRAPS

1

Introduction to Casino Craps

Craps is the fastest and most exciting of all the games offered by the casino, and it's the game in which a gambler can win the most money in the shortest possible time. Each throw of the dice can be a money toss, and payoffs are made continuously.

Although blackjack has more tables devoted to it, and perhaps has more players participating in any casino, it is craps which is the high volume money game, particularly on the Las Vegas Strip, where it's not unusual to find many thousands of dollars being bet on the table at one time, all dependent on one roll of the dice. The action is fast and a ton of money can be won in a short period of time. Anyone coming to the table with a couple of hundred dollars can, with luck and a hot roll, walk away with ten or twenty thousand dollars. It's happened and will continue to happen because that's the kind of game it is. It's fast and loose, and it's a game where winnings can be multiplied quickly.

It is also the traditional game of the big bettors, the high rollers, or premium players, as the casino executives call them. It's

1

a game that moves right along, and one in which money action is predominant. There are no cards to count, no unusual rules to remember. If you play intelligently and correctly, and you catch your hot roll, the chances of making a big win are assured. You'll be a winner.

And that's what this book is all about; winning at craps. The game can be beaten, because with proper strategy, the player gives the house a minimum edge of either 0.8% or 0.6% on most bets, depending on whether single or double free odds are allowed. This relates to a house cut of either 80¢ or 60¢ for each $100 bet, and perhaps the casino deserves this much to run a game for us.

Of course, there are other bets on the table that will give the casino up to 16.67% as its edge, but the wise player will avoid these wagers. This book will show you all kinds of ways to beat the house, to give the casino the slightest of advantages, and then show how to overcome this with smart play, proper money management and self-control. Craps can be beaten; it's been done before by astute players and the game is wide open to be beaten again.

Best of all, if you follow these winning methods and hit a winning streak of tremendous proportions, the casino can't do a damn thing but pay off. They can't stop you from betting, as they can in blackjack, nor can they change the dice. All they can do is sweat out your winning streak and pay off. I've taught the game to high rollers, and when they hit that hot roll, I've seen the sweat pour down the faces of boxmen and pit bosses, as winnings multiplied, as more casino chips were rushed to the table to cover the casino losses, and they couldn't do anything but pay out over and over again.

When you win at casino craps, it's like coining your own money. The casino chips fill your rails, and as the winning streak goes on, these chips turn from $5 into $25 chips, then to $100 chips, and if the streak lasts long enough, into $500 chips. All it takes is one hot roll and you're on your way to big money, and I mean really big money.

After even a moderately good roll of the dice, you'll be making money with the casino's money, and there's nothing the house can do about it. They'll wince and shudder but they'll pay you off. And welcome you again to play, to win still another time.

In writing this book, I realize that the readers will be a diverse group. Some of you will never have played craps before and will know nothing about the game. Others will have played only in street or private games, but never at the casino game. Others will have made some attempt at casino craps, without any real knowledge of the rules or odds, and still others will have had much experience at casino craps. Whatever your level of play, whether rank novice or veteran of the tables, this book will teach you to win.

By the time you finish reading, you're going to know as much about craps as anyone who is involved with the game, and I include casino managers, pit bosses and dealers in this category. Not only that, but this book will reveal methods of play and strategies never before put into print. The purpose of this work is to transmit this knowledge to you, the reader, and to make you a winner.

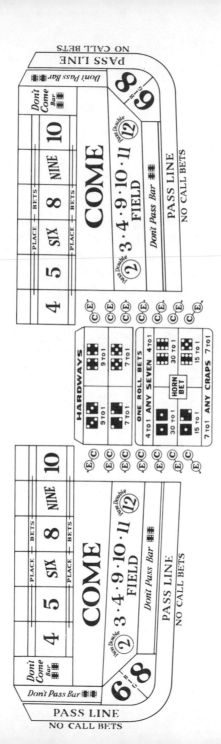

Nevada Layout, Las Vegas

2

The Dice—
Combinations
and Odds

To thoroughly understand the game of craps, it's important to understand the dice and their possible combinations, for these combinations determine all the odds of the game, and ultimately, all the payoffs on all bets.

The game is played with two dice; each die having six sides, with each side imprinted with from one to six dots, so that the lowest number that can be thrown with one die is 1, and the highest, 6. With two dice in operation, the lowest number that can be rolled is 2, and the highest, 12. Together, these two dice are capable of making thirty-six possible combinations of all the numbers ranging from 2 to 12.

Casino dice are special dice, different from the ordinary dice sold with most games or in stores. For one thing casino dice are usually larger than standard dice, measuring about ¾ of an inch on each side, and are as close as possible to exact cubes as modern machinery can make them. They are made of a hard transparent plastic, usually red (though other colors are sometimes used) and have the casino's name and logo imprinted on one side.

Each die usually has a code number as well, for the dice are made to specific order for each casino. The code number of the six or eight dice used for a particular session at the craps table are noted in advance by the boxman, so that no other dice bearing similar design may be introduced by cheats during the game. It is the duty of the boxman to keep track of the dice and examine them, especially when they are thrown or dropped off the table.

He must examine the returned die and twirl it around, checking for the code number and looking for any imperfections hurriedly applied while the die was out of play. The stickman, who is one of the dealers, during the course of a roll continually turns the dice over with his stick, while they are on the table. He does this to make certain that each die is numbered from 1 to 6, because should a foreign set of dice be introduced and numbered only with even numbers, this would prevent a 7 from appearing on the dice, to the great detriment and loss of the casino.

A shooter may select any two dice from about six or eight offered to him at the outset of the roll, and may keep these two dice throughout his roll, even if one or both have temporarily fallen off the table. He may ask for the same dice back, since many shooters want to keep one pair of dice throughout a good roll. Many bettors are superstitious and often all bets are called off on the immediate roll after new dice are introduced. Sometimes the dice are changed at the request of the shooter, for he can do this at any time. Sometimes the fallen die can't be found in time for the next roll, and, to keep the game going, the shooter is obligated to take a new die or dice.

But dice have no memory, and all dice are alike in size and weight, so it is merely a personal idiosyncracy that determines the use of the same dice throughout a roll. Some gamblers don't care what dice they are throwing, and reason that, after a hot roll, the 7 is sure to come soon, so they change dice, thinking that the 7 will take longer with the new dice. This kind of thinking is just as random and unscientific as sticking to one set of dice for the entire roll, but a lot of money is often at stake on each roll, and gamblers do what they can to help themselves, even when none of it makes any sense.

COMBINATIONS OF DICE

The following are the various ways that dice can be rolled:

Number	Combinations
2	1-1
3	1-2, 2-1
4	1-3, 3-1, 2-2
5	1-4, 4-1, 2-3, 3-2
6	1-5, 5-1, 2-4, 4-2, 3-3
7	1-6, 6-1, 2-5, 5-2, 3-4, 4-3
8	2-6, 6-2, 3-5, 5-3, 4-4
9	3-6, 6-3, 4-5, 5-4
10	4-6, 6-4, 5-5
11	5-6, 6-5
12	6-6

Looking at the above table of combinations, we see that there is a definite symmetrical curve, with both 2 and 12 made with only one combination, and the 7, in the center, made with six combinations.

A 7 can be rolled no matter what number is on one die, for it can accommodate both the 6 and the 1, which no other number can do. A 6 cannot be rolled with a 6 showing on one die, and an 8 cannot be rolled with a 1 showing. The key number in dice is 7, and it determines most of the odds of the game because of its unique status as a winner on the come-out roll, and a loser against an established point.

The other important thing about the 7 is that all the point numbers are measured against it in determining the true odds against repeating these numbers.

These point numbers are 4, 5, 6, 8, 9 and 10. If any of these numbers are rolled, and bet on the come-out or afterward as a come or place number, the odds are always against that number repeating before a 7 is rolled.

The following table shows the odds against repeating any of these numbers before a 7 shows on the dice. All odds are determined by the fact that the 7 can be rolled in six possible ways.

Number	Ways to Roll	Odds Against Repeating Before a 7 Is Rolled
4	3	2-1
5	4	3-2
6	5	6-5
8	5	6-5
9	4	3-2
10	3	2-1

There are other bets on the casino layout, and some may be made on one-roll propositions. In this case, a player is betting that a particular number will show on the very next roll of the dice. The following table shows the true odds against any of these numbers occurring on the very next roll.

Number	Ways to Roll	True Odds Against on Any Single Roll
2	1	35-1
3	2	17-1
7	6	5-1
11	2	17-1
12	1	35-1

3

The Casino Craps Layout

The layout, to define it simply, is the printed arrangement of boxes, spaces and areas showing the various types of bets permitted by the casino at which the player is gambling. This imprint of words and symbols is made on the felt surface of the craps table that the players stand around so they can look down with ease at the betting surface. All bets made by the players are placed on this layout.

Most layouts are printed in white on green felt, but although this is fairly standard, there is no real uniformity among casinos. Some will have yellow printing on green felt, and still other casinos will have different color arrangements. The Las Vegas Hilton, for example, uses a blue felt cover for its craps tables, in keeping with its general decor. The Holiday Casino in Las Vegas uses an eye-jarring red as its felt color.

Generally, green seems to be the best color for a layout surface because it's soothing, and the human eye has a tendency to see everything in motion when other colors are used, which can become quite disconcerting. If a gambler is at a table where other colors predominate, he may get fatigued in a short while as a result of both the obtrusive color he faces and the great deal of smoke and noise found in any casino.

The following is a complete craps layout:

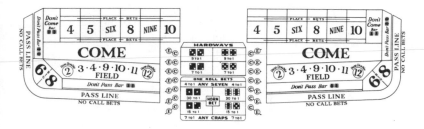

Nevada Layout, Las Vegas

We can see that the layout is divided into three distinct parts. The two end sections are identical, and between them is a betting area known as the center. This center betting section contains the proposition, hardway, and other wagers under the domain and control of the stickman. All the bets that can be made in this section will be covered at length in the appropriate section of this book, but none of these center bets are worthwhile for the astute player, since the house edge is too high.

Each of the side or end sections is controlled and operated by a standing dealer. These sections contain most of the important bets on the layout, and each of them will be discussed fully in later chapters.

Some of the most important bets that are made on the layout include the pass-line bet, made by about 90% of the players on the come-out roll; the come bet, favored by right bettors after the point is established, and the place numbers, which are also heavily bet. The place numbers are those in order on top of each side section— 4, 5, six, 8, nine and 10. These numbered boxes are also the repository for come and don't come bets after they have been removed from the appropriate betting boxes. Again, all this will be further explained in the appropriate chapters.

The don't come and don't pass betting areas are smaller than their counterparts, the come and pass-line areas, because fewer bettors wage money on them during the course of a game.

Field bets take up a great deal of space on the layout, an inordinate amount actually, for these bets get little play from astute gamblers. These are one-roll bets, paid off or lost after each roll of the dice, and are usually played by the ignorant, uninitiated or systems players. They get so much space because the house advantage on these wagers is quite high.

A great deal of space is also given to the Big 6 and Big 8 bets, but these are poor bets for the player and should always be avoided. Whenever I see anyone making a Big 6 or Big 8 bet, I know that he or she has no knowledge of the game.

Again, these bets will be fully discussed in later chapters. What is not shown on the layout is a wager which plays an important part of any winning strategy, the free odds bet. This bet can be made with any pass-line or don't pass bet after a point is established. It can be made with a come or don't come bet, but for some reason (perhaps greed) this bet is not shown on the layout. However, it will be fully discussed so that the player can take advantage of free odds.

The layout shown here is roughly what the player will see in any casino he goes into. There might be some slight modification, some slight variant in payoffs, but all bets here can be made in any casino in Nevada and Atlantic City.

OTHER LAYOUTS

In some casinos, usually in foreign jurisdictions or in private illegal establishments, there are other types of layouts used. The most common difference between these and the standard one we described is the absence of a Come Bet. When these bets are not available, the right bettor must make place bets rather than come bets, at a disadvantage to himself.

In some casinos, the 6 and 8 cannot be bet even as a place bet, only as a Big 6 or Big 8, and again, this puts the bettor at a great disadvantage.

I mention these other layouts only in passing, because once you understand how to bet at the standard layout, you can prepare yourself to play in any legitimate casino in America, and if playing in a foreign country, you will know exactly what bets to avoid on unfamiliar layouts.

4

The Fundamentals of Casino Craps

CRAPS TABLES AND BETTING LIMITS

The average casino craps table is about the size of a large billiard table and can accommodate between twelve and twenty-four players. The tables vary in size but the size differential is slight and unimportant to the player, except in terms of convenience.

In casinos with more than one craps table, each table is numbered, for the casino's convenience, with designations such as "Craps 1," "Craps 2," etc. Usually the largest of the hotel casinos rarely has more than six craps tables, and it is unusual to find them all in operation except on crowded nights, holidays and weekends.

Craps 1 is the lead table in most casinos, and it is always open. As business increases, other tables open, and as they get crowded, still others may be put into operation. The casino personnel prefer two very crowded tables to four half-empty ones, for they feel that players are attracted to noisy and busy games. They don't like dead tables with only a couple of small bettors hanging around.

The more crowded the table, the larger the betting seems to get, because players loosen up among other players. A camaraderie seems to develop at a table while the game is in full swing, since 90% of the players bet with the dice, and thus, their goals are the same and everyone is rooting for the dice to pass.

When only one table is open in a Las Vegas Strip casino, the limits generally range from $1 minimum to $500 maximum. As more tables open up, the minimum limit may go up to $5 at some tables. The maximum limit usually remains at $500, however, but again, this rule is flexible and may rise to $1,000 during crowded periods of play. But $1,000 is usually the maximum limit on line bets at any Nevada casino, with few exceptions. When the limit is $1,000, a player may still bet another $1,000 as a single odds bet, or $2,000 as a double odds bet behind the line, and if he bets all the come bets the same way, he can have as much as $21,000 on the table at one time, which certainly is not small change.

A casino limits the maximum bets because it would rather grind out players with its overall advantage on most bets than see a couple of hours of hot rolls beat the casino for a small fortune. Only certain casinos allow double odds bets (which will be fully explained later on) because a hot roll can really hurt a casino. I personally know of one casino where a shooter got a hot hand and with a table full of high rollers took the casino for close to a half-million dollars in a few hours. That loss sobered the casino, which was having financial problems, and it prohibited double odds after that ghastly experience.

Some casino operators are not afraid of big bettors, however, and will accommodate *any bettor and any limit*. Benny Binion, for example, who runs the Horseshoe Club in downtown Las Vegas, has no maximum betting limit on his craps tables. You set your own limit by your first bet. If you put down $100,000 on the pass-line right away, that's your limit from then on. But not many operators have followed his example, and Benny Binion is unique in Las Vegas in terms of the gambles he'll take against players.

Expect to face a $500 limit when you play at the average

casino. If double odds are allowed, you can bet $1,000 behind the line as well, and if single odds are permitted, you may only bet an additional $500 behind the line. While this may seem like a great deal to bet at any one time, you may find that when you get involved in a hot shoot and keep raising your bets, if the shoot lasts long enough, you might soon be bucking that limit.

If you want to raise the betting limits, ask the boxman to increase them. He'll speak to the pitboss, and may very well let you go beyond the house limit. But this is discretionary with the casino operators. However, if you've been killing the casino, you'll probably get your wish, for the only way they can get back their money during your play is for you to lose some big bets.

In the downtown Las Vegas casinos and in casinos around Nevada, there are lower minimum limits for craps tables, and you can find, if you're so inclined, many 25¢ minimum games. But even here, the maximum bet allowed will be $500. Always ask the limits before you play if you don't see them posted, for you don't want to get into a bigger game than you can afford. Also, many players don't like to play at 25¢ games when they're betting big bucks.

CASINO CHIPS

The casino game of craps is not played with cash, but with casino checks, called chips by most players. We'll also call them chips, to differentiate them from bank checks. Chips come in various standard denominations, of $1, $5, $25, $100 and $500. In most casinos the Eisenhower dollar is used in place of $1 chips. And in the cheap games there are also 25¢ chips as well.

There are no standard colors for the various denominations, but usually $5 chips are red or reddish brown, $25 chips are green, and $100 chips are black or black and yellow. Even these colors aren't constant. In the Dunes in Las Vegas the $500 chips are pink, while in the Horseshoe, these same chips are gray. It's up to the various casinos to select and color their own chips.

It's possible to bet cash at a table, but the casino discourages this, and even if you bet cash by saying "cash plays," you'll be paid off with casino chips. The casino wants the cash in the drop box located under each craps table, and not on the table.

It doesn't want cash for two reasons. First, cash is clumsy, since all bills are the same color and have to be carefully examined and counted time and time again. Secondly, for most players chips are an abstraction, while cash buys goods and services; therefore, if a player loses chips, he doesn't feel as bad as if he were losing cold cash. He thus has a tendency to make bigger bets with chips.

Once you get to a table, you should change your cash into chips. The easy way is to hand over the cash to the dealer, who will give it to the boxman to count. Then the dealer will ask you what denominations of chips you want and will then give you a stack of casino chips.

After you receive your chips, you should immediately put them into the grooved rails made expressly to fit the chips. These rails run the length of the table, and every player has his own area, separated from his neighbors by a cross insert of plastic or wood.

It's the duty of each player to watch over his chips and protect them during the course of the game. Thievery among craps players is rare but it does occur at times. You should always be alert because these chips are the equivalent of money and are valuable.

CREDIT

Many big bettors don't play with or bring cash to the tables. They have established credit at the casino and ask for credit at the table. They do this by signing "markers" which are IOUs. For example, you may come to the table and ask the dealer for a $500 marker. The dealer will turn to the boxman, who, if he recognizes you, will accede to your request.

If he doesn't know you, or is unsure about your credit, a floorman will be called over, to give his O.K. for credit. If the floorman is unsure of you, he will ask your name, and a call will be made from the craps pit by the pit bookkeeper to check on your credit at the casino. If your credit is good, you'll be given $500 in chips, sign a marker, and then play with the chips.

Once the session is over, if you have won, you will be asked to repay the marker immediately, before leaving the table. The house doesn't care to extend credit when it can be paid back, for it has enough trouble with losers and their credit.

You can establish credit beforehand by filling out an application form with a casino in which you disclose pertinent financial information about yourself, such as bank balances and references. If credit is approved, a certain ceiling is established and you may take credit up to that amount. If you are a loser, the casino will accept your check in payment for your losses.

If you don't have credit then you must bring cash to the casino. Don't expect to come to a casino and get instant credit. It takes time to establish it, and if you want to play and don't have credit, you better bring real money with you.

CASINO PERSONNEL

The casino craps table is staffed by a minimum of four employees at any one time. Three of them stand and one sits. The standing men are the dealers, dressed in the uniform of the casino. The sitting man is dressed in a sports jacket or suit, and he is known as the boxman.

There are three shifts in a twenty-four-hour period called the day, swing and graveyard shifts, and each lasts eight hours. On any one shift, four dealers, called a "crew," work. Three are at the table, and the fourth is on a break. The dealers take turns staffing the table and taking their breaks. Also, each dealer moves around the table, taking turns at various positions. The standing dealers who face the players are said to be "on base," while the third dealer, known as the stickman, is said to be "on the stick."

The seated boxman is not really part of this crew. His job is to oversee the table as a whole, count the cash as it comes in, and make decisions when there is a dispute between a dealer and a player. When such a dispute occurs, if it is for a small amount, the player will get the benefit of the doubt.

Sometimes at a crowded table with a lot of money action, there are two seated boxmen, one to watch each side of the table. They sit between the standing dealers, and face the stickman.

One of the standing dealers is the person with whom you'll be dealing directly during the course of your play. Each standing dealer has specific duties.

1. He will convert your cash into casino chips, and will "change color," or change chips into larger or smaller denominations at your request. When asking for chips, an experienced player asks for nickels instead of $5 chips, and quarters, instead of $25 chips.

2. He pays off all winning line bets, and collects all losing line bets. He also pays off any other winning bets and collects any losing bets, other than the center layout bets.

3. He handles all place bets and puts all come and don't come bets into the proper place box numbers, and returns these bets when they are taken down after a particular roll.

4. After a point is established on the come-out roll, he moves a large plastic disk to the box number on the layout to indicate the point.

These plastic disks are usually colored black and white. When it is on the black side, there is no point number established and the disk rests near the dealer, usually in the don't come box. When a point has been established, it is turned over to its white side and placed in the appropriate box number. For example, if the point is 6, it is moved into the 6 box number.

The stickman, who doesn't deal directly with the players except when collecting bets on the center portion of the layout, has his duties as well:

1. When a new shooter is coming out, the stickman pushes all the available dice over to the shooter, so that he may select two to roll with.

2. After each roll of the dice, the stickman calls the number rolled and indicates whether or not it is a winner. For example, if the point is 5, and a 5 is rolled, he will say "Five, winner on the pass-line." If a 2 is rolled on the come-out roll, he will say "Two, a craps, loser on the pass-line."

3. He handles all wagers on any bets made on the center of the layout. If the bet loses, he picks up the chips and gives them to the boxman. If the bet wins, the stickman notifies the appropriate dealer to pay off the winning bettor.

4. He keeps a continuous spiel going during the play. Before the come-out roll, a stickman might say "New shooter coming out, bet those hardways, bet the field, get those bets down on craps, eleven." After a point is established, the stickman will say, "Point is 6, it came easy, bet it hard, make it come out." And during the roll he will continually push his center bets, which are very favorable bets for the house, by saying, "Bet the hardways, bet any craps, who'll bet craps, eleven?"

A good stickman can "talk up" a game, and make it very lively, getting the players to make all kinds of foolish bets and to constantly increase their wagers. He will always ask for hardway bets, because many of those bets are made as tips, or tokes, for the dealers. And he will root for the shooter, saying, for example, "Make that point, shooter, have that point come out," because when there's a hot roll going, bets increase dramatically, as do the dealer's tokes.

Not all stickmen are good talkers. Some merely call the game, announcing the last roll, and that's all, and others, due to casino policy, never root for the shooter. Some casino personnel are so superstitious that they believe rooting for the point hurts the house and will make the number appear on the dice.

The boxman's duties are as follows:

1. He collects all hard cash and places it in a dropbox below the table, by sliding the money into an opening with a wooden paddle.

2. He is in charge of the table, watching every move of the dealers. He makes certain that the payoffs are correct and that the dealers collect all losing bets.

3. He settles any disputes between dealer and player. If a player disagrees with his decision, the player may appeal to a floorman, and ultimately, to the pitboss.

4. If a die or both dice have been thrown or fall off the table, he examines the dice before returning them to the game. He makes certain that they are house dice and haven't been tampered with.

Craps tables are arranged so that they enclose an area known as the "craps pit." In charge of the entire pit is the pitboss who has general supervisory duties involving all the personnel under his direction.

Floormen, who are directly below the pitboss in authority, are assigned to particular tables. They watch the game for any unusual activity or cheating and, in addition, they watch and check on the junket members' action, taking notes on their bets, their time at the table, etc.

Floormen are also in charge of extending credit to players and checking on the status of any player's credit. The floorman makes certain that the player signs a marker for chips received. Sometimes a floorman sits in a chair overlooking the table, and is known as a "ladderman." This practice is rare, but still occurs in certain casinos, such as The Four Queens, in downtown Las Vegas.

Aiding the floorman is a pit bookkeeper who either calls the cashier's cage to check on a player's credit or tunes into a computer, which instantly shows the player's outstanding balance and open credit.

Also there may be unobserved security personnel, such as private detectives and the "eye in the sky"—the men behind the one-way mirrors over every craps table who watch the action at the table closely, making certain that the game moves along honestly and smoothly.

THE SHOOTER

Every player has the right to shoot the dice and become the "shooter" when it is his turn to do so. The shoot goes around the table in clockwise fashion. All the players at the game are bound by the rolls of the shooter and win or lose their bets depending upon what number he throws.

When it is your turn to roll the dice, you must make a line bet—either pass or don't pass. It's rare for anyone to make a don't pass bet when holding the dice, for very few players want to bet against their own roll. Even players who are notorious wrong bettors will switch to the pass-line when on a shoot. Some don't pass bettors simply give up the dice when it is their turn to roll the dice. Any player may refuse to shoot the dice.

When you are designated as the shooter, you select two of the dice the stickman offers from the dice box which usually contains between four and eight dice.

After you have selected your dice and made your line bet, shake the dice, preparing to roll them. They should be thrown so that both hit the far end of the table, giving them a random bounce. However, if they don't go that far on the table, it still will be a good roll unless the boxman decides that the roll was so weak as not to constitute a fair throw of the dice. In such cases he may call the roll off by saying "no roll."

If either die is thrown off the table or lands up on the rails, the roll is "off" and will not be counted as a legitimate roll. In that case, the stickman will announce "no roll" and all bets will be off.

If the dice or either die lands on a chip or against the wall of the table and leans at an angle, the most horizontal of the numbers is counted as the rolled number. It is not an "off roll." However, if the number cannot be ascertained, it will be considered an off roll by the boxman.

A shooter holds the dice until he "sevens out," that is, until a 7 is rolled after a point has been established on the come-out roll. Even if you "crap out," by rolling a losing pass-line number, such as 2, 3 or 12, you still retain the dice. Only after you seven out or "miss" do you give up the dice.

However, you may relinquish the dice voluntarily just before any come-out roll, but not during a roll where a point has already been established.

A new player arriving at the table may take any open spot available and may select a space where it is his turn to roll the dice. There are no priorities at a craps table. Everyone, in the order in which he is standing, has a turn at shooting the dice.

THE COME-OUT ROLL—THE BASIC GAME

The initial roll of the dice by a new shooter, or the first roll after a point number has been repeated or a craps thrown by an ongoing shooter, is called the come-out roll.

On the come-out roll, the following rules apply:

1. If a shooter rolls a 7 or 11, all the pass-line bettors, that is, those players who bet right, or with the dice, win their bets immediately at even-money. All those who bet against the dice, the wrong or don't pass bettors, lose their bets at once.

2. If a shooter rolls a 2, 3 or 12 (craps) all the pass-line bettors lose their bets, and the wrong bettors win on the 2 and 3. There is a standoff on the 12, however, since it is barred as a winner for the don't pass bettors. This is done to preserve the house advantage over wrong bettors.

In some casinos and in Northern Nevada the 2 is barred to the don't pass bettors instead of the 12. Since either number can only be made with one combination of the dice, the house edge remains the same.

3. After a shooter has rolled a 7 or 11 or a craps on the come-

out roll, there is a new come-out roll, and the shooter and the players can make fresh pass-line or don't pass bets.

4. If any other number is rolled on the come-out roll, either a 4, 5, 6, 8, 9 or 10, that number is called the "point" and must be repeated before a 7 is rolled for the pass-line bettors to win their bets. If the point is repeated, then the don't pass players lose their bets.

5. If the 7 shows before the point is repeated, the don't pass bettors win, and the pass-line bettors lose their bets.

This is the basic game of casino craps. There are many other bets that can be made, either on the come-out roll or afterwards, and all these bets will be discussed in the appropriate chapter of this book.

5

The Line Bets—
with Free Odds

The line bets are the heart of the game of craps for they involve the basic game as it has been played for thousands of years. There are two types of line bets: pass-line and don't pass.

A pass-line bet is made by the right bettor, who hopes the dice will pass or win; and the don't pass bet is made by the wrong bettor, who wants the dice to lose or not pass. The house books both bets, and pays off or collects on them. Some players are under the misconception that betting with the dice is betting against the house and betting against the dice is betting with the casino, but this is not the case. The casino books all bets at a craps table, thus all bets are theoretically against the house.

The most popular bet by far is the pass-line wager for most players, perhaps 90% of them, bet with the dice—betting right. When we use the term "right" we're making no moral judgment. Pass-line bettors are known as "right bettors" and don't pass bettors are known commonly as "wrong bettors."

Since the most common of all bets is a pass-line bet, that's the first wager on the layout that I'll discuss fully.

PASS-LINE BET

Running the length of each end section of the layout is the pass-line. It's there to accommodate all the players at that end of the table who wish to bet with the dice, betting that they will pass.

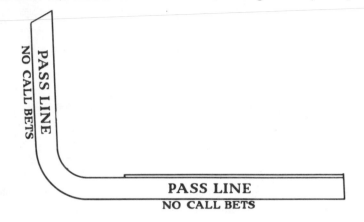

A pass-line bet can only be made on the come-out roll, and, as discussed previously, a come-out roll occurs in three different instances. First, there is a come-out roll when a new shooter handles the dice and prepares for the first or initial roll. It occurs when, on that initial roll, the shooter has rolled a 7, 11, 2, 3 or 12. The 7 and 11 are immediate winners, and the 2, 3 and 12 are immediate losers for the pass-line bettors, and their bets are either paid off or collected after these numbers are rolled. Finally, there is a come-out roll after the shooter has made the point by repeating it before a 7 comes up on the dice. Let's explore all these terms in greater depth.

On the come-out roll, if you roll a 7 or 11, you roll a winner for the pass-line or right bettors and their bets are paid off at once at even-money. However, if on the come-out roll you roll a 2, 3 or 12, all called "craps," the pass-line bettors lose their wagers immediately and they are removed from the layout by the dealer.

If any other number is rolled on the come-out roll—4, 5, 6, 8, 9 or 10, that number is known as the "point." This point must be repeated before a 7 is rolled in order for the pass-line bettors to win their bets.

For example, if a 6 is rolled on the come-out, the 6 must be repeated before a 7 shows for the pass-line bettor to win. Suppose the sequence of numbers were as follows:

Come-out roll—6. That is the point. Then 5, 9, 10, 2, 3, 5, 11, 12, 6.

Once the second 6 was rolled, the point repeated and the pass-line players won their bets. The other numbers had no relevance whatsoever to this ultimate determination. Let's now summarize this information.

1. On the come-out roll, if a 7 or 11 is rolled, it is an immediate win for pass-line bettors, at even-money.

2. If a 2, 3 or 12 (craps) is rolled, it is an immediate loser for these bettors, on the come-out roll.

3. If, on the come-out roll, a 4, 5, 6, 8, 9 or 10 is rolled, the number rolled is known as the point.

4. If the point is repeated before a 7 is rolled, the pass-line bettors win their bets, and are paid off at even-money for their line bets.

5. If a 7 comes up before the point is repeated, the pass-line bettors lose, and their chips are removed from the layout.

Any number, other than the point or 7, rolled between the establishment of the point and either its repeat or a 7, is immaterial to the ultimate decision of the pass-line bet.

FREE ODDS BETS

We now come to the most important bet allowed at the craps table—one which the astute and intelligent player will make much use of. This is the "free odds" bet. If we look over the complete casino craps layout, we won't find any such bet listed, but it is allowed, nevertheless, in all American casinos.

I'll explain the concept of a free odds bet carefully, for it is one that many craps players don't truly understand. A free odds bet is a wager that a player may make after a point has been established on the come-out roll. This bet can be made equal to the amount bet on the pass-line. For example, if you had wagered $10 on the pass-line and the come-out roll was a 6 (the point), you may now bet an additional $10 as a single odds bet at the correct odds of 6-5 on the 6.

You make this bet by putting the chips behind the original bet. If we look back on the illustration of the pass-line, there is a statement "no call bets" shown. It is in this area, just behind the pass-line, that the odds bet is placed. Because the bet is made behind the pass-line, it is also called a "behind the line" bet. By making this wager, you are "taking" odds on the point on which you are wagering.

The following are the free odds paid on the point numbers:

Number	Odds
4 or 10	2-1
5 or 9	3-2
6 or 8	6-5

The payoffs are determined by mathematics. Since there are six ways to roll a 7, and only three ways to roll a 4 or 10, the odds against a 4 or 10 repeating before a 7 is rolled is 2-1. Since there are four ways to roll either a 5 or 9, the odds against either of these numbers repeating before the 7 comes up is 3-2. And a 6 or 8 can be rolled five ways; so the odds against either number is 6-5.

If you win your bet, you will be paid even-money on your pass-line bet and the correct odds on your behind-the-line bet. For example, if the point were a 6, and you wagered $10 on the pass-line and $10 as an odds bet and won, you'd be paid $10 for the line bet and $12 for the odds bet, at 6-5, or $12-$10.

The house has no advantage over the player on any free odds bet and it is the only bet on the entire layout where this is so. Whenever possible, you should make free odds bets.

The house has an advantage of approximately 1.4% on the pass-line bet without free odds. With a single odds bet, this advantage is reduced to 0.8%. When you are allowed to make a free odds bet double the original pass-line bet (called *double odds)* the house edge drops to 0.6% over the player. Here's how a double odds bet is made: Suppose you have bet $10 on the pass-line and the point is 6. You may now bet double your pass-line bet, or $20, on the free odds bet at 6-5. If the point is repeated before a 7 comes up, you will win $10 for your line bet at even-money and $24 for your odds bet at 6-5, or $24-$20. Of course, if the point is not made and a 7 shows, you will lose both your line and odds bets.

If you have bet $5 on the pass-line, you are permitted to make a single odds bet of $5 on the 4, 6, 8 and 10, but may bet $6 on the 5 and 9 should they be the points. This is permitted since the house will not pay off in half-dollars and the correct odds are really 7½-5. By betting $6, you will receive $9 as your payoff if the point is made.

Although a free odds bet can be removed at any time at the player's option, these odds bets should never be removed since the house has no advantage on these wagers. Remember: having a free odds bet in addition to a regular pass-line bet reduces the house advantage to 0.8% with single odds, and 0.6% with double odds.

Let's now follow a series of rolls to see how you should handle your line bets with free odds. In this theoretical situation, the casino offers only single odds and you will bet a steady $10 on the pass-line.

Come-out roll	3	$10 loss because a craps was rolled on the come-out roll
New come-out roll	5	$10 bet plus $10 odds at 3-2 on the 5, which is the point
Next rolls	9, 4, 3, 11	These rolls don't affect the pass-line bet
Next roll	5	You win $10 at even-money on your pass-line bet and $15 on your free odds bet at 3-2
New come-out roll	11	$10 win on the pass-line
New come-out roll	8	$10 bet plus $10 odds at 6-5 on the 8, which is now the point
Next rolls	5, 6, 4, 2	These rolls don't affect the pass-line bet
Next roll	7	You lose both your pass-line and odds bets because the 7 was rolled before the point was made, for a loss of $20

There is now a new come-out roll with a new shooter and, once again, you will bet $10 on the pass-line. Although odds bets may be removed at any time, the pass-line bet, once made, cannot be removed.

DON'T PASS BET

This betting area is much smaller than the pass-line.

Don't Pass Bar ⬚⬚

The reason for this difference in size is familiar to anyone who has ever played casino craps. The vast majority of players bet with the dice by placing their chips on the pass-line. There are several reasons for this inclination.

First, when betting pass-line and free odds, more money is returned to the bettor than he puts out if he wins his bet.

Secondly, right bettors don't stop with pass-line wagers. They might continue to bet with the dice on place numbers or come bets, with odds, and, therefore, they'll be getting back more money than they've wagered if they win any of these additional bets. Also, by betting right they can be the recipients of a "hot roll," where numbers continually show on the dice enabling them to win continually as each number repeats.

Thirdly, there is the psychological aspect of right betting. By betting with the dice, the pass-line player is betting with the crowd. He has something in common with most of the other gamblers at the table. They want to see the dice pass and they want to see numbers repeat. Above all, they want that hot roll to develop.

Still another factor enters into the picture. I've interviewed many craps players and found that the pass-line bettors at the table feel they're optimists, rather than pessimists, when they bet with the dice. Even the connotations of right and wrong bettors have psychological overtones, though literally speaking, they mean nothing. Betting right is betting the dice will pass and betting wrong means wagering against the dice. It really has nothing to do with optimism or morality.

And whether you bet with the dice or against them, the odds are pretty much the same. The difference is minute, and actually favors the wrong bettor—1.40% to 1.41%.

At any craps table, on average, there are never more than one or two players betting don't pass. The rest of the gamblers are betting pass-line. When the dice are cold, no points are being made, and all the pass-line and right bettors are losing, they look sideways with hate in their eyes at the winning wrong bettors. The right and pass-line bettors secretly hope for a hot roll, not only to make money for themselves, but to destroy what they regard as the smug don't pass bettors who are cleaning up. Usually the don't pass bettor is a loner, apart from the crowd, his wishes diametrically opposed to the majority of players at the table.

Because a gambler can make money betting the don't pass line as well as the pass-line, I feel that you should be prepared to bet either way and not close your mind to wrong betting. In fact, in discussing winning strategies later in this book, I'll show how to make money either way.

It should also be pointed out that the most famous craps player of all time, the legendary Nick the Greek, was a wrong bettor, and almost always bet don't pass. So, it isn't just the peculiar bettor who wagers against the dice.

Let's examine the mechanics of betting against the dice. First, you will make your usual $10 bet by placing the chips in the don't pass area just before the come-out roll.

If a 2 or 3 is rolled you will immediately win your bet. If a 12 is rolled (in Northern Nevada a 2), it is a standoff and you neither lose nor win. This is what is meant by the expression that the "12 is barred" on the layout. If the 12 weren't barred to the wrong bettor, he'd actually have an edge over the casino. Since the 12 can only be made by one combination of the dice, and the 2 can also be made by one combination, it doesn't really matter which number is barred to the wrong bettor, for the odds remain the same.

If, on the come-out roll, a 7 or 11 is rolled, this is an immediate loser for you on the don't pass line.

To summarize: on all come-out rolls, for the wrong bettor,

1. If a 2 or 3 is rolled   Immediate win
2. If a 12 is rolled   Standoff
3. If a 7 or 11 is rolled   Immediate loss

If any other number is rolled, either a 4, 5, 6, 8, 9 or 10 on the come-out roll, that is the point. If the point is made before a 7 shows on the dice, you, as the don't pass bettor would lose your bet, along with your odds bet. If a 7 is rolled before the point is repeated, then you would win your bet, along with your odds bet.

FREE ODDS

Like the pass-line bettor, the don't pass player has the right to make a free odds bet; but, whereas the right bettor takes odds at better than even-money, the don't pass bettor must *lay* odds at less than even-money. In effect, the don't pass bettor is putting out more money on a free odds bet than he will receive if he wins his bet. Let's now recapitulate the odds against making various point numbers:

4 or 10	2-1
5 or 9	3-2
6 or 8	6-5

If the point is a 4 or 10 and you, as the pass-line bettor, have bet $10 on the don't pass, you now can lay $20 on the free odds bet at 2-1. If you win the bet, you will collect $10 at even-money on your line bet, and $10 at 1-2 on your free odds bet.

If the point was 5 or 9 you'd lay $15-$10. And if you won the bet, you'd collect $10 on your line bet, and $10 on your free odds bet at 2-3.

Finally, if the point was a 6 or 8, you'd have to lay $12 on the free odds bet at 6-5. If you won your bets, again you'd collect only $20 for your combined line and odds bet.

Not many gamblers like to lay odds. They'd rather collect more than they've put on the table. We should remember, however, that the casino books all bets and the house, therefore, books mostly right bettors' wagers and makes most of its payoffs at better than even-money. Despite this fact, casinos make enormous profits from their craps tables.

When single odds bets are made by don't pass bettors, the

house advantage drops from 1.4% to approximately 0.8%. When double odds are permitted, the casino edge drops even further, to 0.6%. Here's how double odds would be bet:

If you have bet $10 on the don't pass line, you can now bet $40-$20 if the point is a 4 or 10.

If the point is a 5 or 9, you may bet $30-$20 as your double free odds bet. And if the point is a 6 or 8, you may lay $24-$20 as your free odds bet.

When laying odds, you, as the don't pass bettor, place the additional chips not behind the line, but either on top of your don't pass bet at a slight tilt or alongside your don't pass bet, as illustrated:

Odds bets may be removed at any time by the wrong bettor, but it's to your advantage to lay odds, and you shouldn't remove them once they've been made. In fact, the don't pass bet can also be removed at any time by the player, but again, since it does favor the wrong bettor once a point has been established, it should never be taken down.

Let's now follow a sample roll of the dice to fully understand don't pass betting with free odds. You are at a single odds casino and are betting $10 on the don't pass line.

Come-out roll	3	$10 win for you
New come-out roll	5	$10 plus $15 odds bet against the 5 at 3-2
Next rolls	6, 8, 10	These rolls have no effect on the don't pass bet
Next roll	7	You win $10 on your line bet, and $10 on your odds bet, for a total win of $20

New shooter coming out		
New come-out roll	12	A standoff. The 12 is barred as a winning bet for the wrong bettor
New come-out roll	7	$10 loss for the don't pass bettor
New come-out roll	10	$10 plus $20 odds bet against the 10 at 2-1

And the roll continues.

On the come-out roll, the pass-line bettor has eight chances for an immediate win; six with the 7 and two with the 11. You, the don't pass bettor, can only win with three combinations of the dice; two with the 3 and one with the 2.

However, once the point is established, you have an advantage on every point number ranging from 6-5 on the 6 and 8, to 3-2 on the 5 or 9, and to 2-1 on the 4 and 10.

Nevertheless, whether betting pass-line or don't pass, you gamble at almost the same disadvantage, approximately 1.4% on line bets without odds, 0.8% with single odds, and 0.6% with double odds.

6

Come and Don't Come Bets— with Free Odds

COME BETS

Come bets are the most misunderstood bets on the craps layout, perhaps because the word "come" means nothing to the average craps player. What exactly is a come bet? To define it simply, a come bet is any bet made after the come-out roll betting with the dice, in the same manner as a pass-line bet. If a 7 or 11 is rolled, it's an immediate winner on the come bet; if a 2, 3 or 12 is rolled, it's an immediate loser; and if any point number is rolled, that number must be repeated before a 7 shows on the dice for the come bettor to win.

The one difference between a come bet and a pass-line bet, then, is that the come bet can only be made after the come-out roll, while a pass-line bet is made on the come-out roll. Otherwise, they're the same bets, winning and losing the same way.

A come bet serves two purposes: one for the house and one for the player. For the house, it permits continual betting on every roll of the dice by the right bettor, ensuring that more money will be bet on the layout. The more money bet, the more the casino's potential profit, for it has an edge on this bet just as it has on every bet in the layout with the exception of the free odds bet.

The advantage to you is that you can keep making right bets with free odds at the same low house edge of 0.8% with single odds bets and 0.6% if double odds are permitted. If the point and come numbers start repeating and the roll turns into a hot one, then you can make a small fortune in a very short period of time. You're giving the house little in the way of an edge, and with some luck, you have the opportunity of overcoming the edge in a short series of rolls while getting compound interest, as it were, on your bets.

Once a point has been established on the come-out roll, you can make your come bet by placing your chips in the come box. Suppose you make a $10 bet. If the next roll is a 7 or 11, you immediately win your come bet. If the roll is a 7, you lose your pass-line bet, but the come bet is completely different.

If a 2, 3 or 12 is rolled, you'd lose your come bet and it wouldn't affect your pass-line bet. If the roll was a point number, that would be your come number. It would have to be repeated before a 7 was rolled for you to win your come bet, without affecting the pass-line bet. If the point number rolled was the same as the point, the pass-line bet would win, but still this wouldn't affect the come bet.

Let's assume that the point was 9 on the come-out roll. After you placed $10 in the come box, the next roll of the dice was a 6. At this point, the $10 in chips would be removed from the come box by the dealer and put into the center of the place box number 6. You can now give the dealer an additional $10 as single odds, which will be placed at a tilt on the $10 come bet already resting in the place number 6 box. It is slightly tilted to indicate that the additional bet is at odds.

You are not limited to only one come bet, but can continually make them on every roll of the dice. You can make another come bet by again placing $10 in the come box. If the next roll is a 5. The dealer removes the $10 and puts these chips in the 5 place box. Just as before, by giving the dealer $10 additional in chips and stating that these are "odds," you have these chips placed on the original come bet on the 5 at a slight tilt.

Let's now summarize the preceding bets:

Come-out roll	9 (point)	$10 on pass-line and $10 odds
First come roll	6	$10 as come bet and $10 odds
Second come roll	5	$10 as come bet and $10 odds

At this moment, you have three numbers "working" for you. You have $60 on the layout, $30 in line and come bets, and $30 additional in odds bets. What you want is for these numbers to repeat. What you don't want is the nightmare of all right bettors after all these bets have been established—a 7. If a 7 is rolled, you lose all bets, including the free odds bets. But, if any of your numbers repeat, you will be paid off at better than even-money. Let's continue this theoretical roll and follow it to the end.

Next roll	8	It doesn't affect your bets
Next roll	3	Again, no effect on the bets
Next roll	5	The 5 come bet wins. The dealer will first pay you $25; $10 for your come bet and $15 for your winning odds bet, at 3-2

After a come bet has repeated, if there is no new bet in the come box, the bet is taken down and returned to the player. At this time, the dealer hands over $20 to you in addition to your wins.

There is no longer a come bet on the 5, and if you want another come bet working, you will have to make another wager in the come box. Since you want two come bets working, you now make another $10 bet in the come box, and the roll continues.

Next roll	7	$10 come bet in come box is a winner and is paid off, but both the pass-line bet and come bet on the 6 are losers, together with the odds, since a 7 came up before either of these numbers repeated

Let's summarize the wins and losses on this particular roll:

5 repeated as come bet with odds	Win $25
7 wins as come bet	Win $10
9 loses as pass-line bet with odds	Lose $20
6 loses as come bet with odds	Lose $20
	Net Loss $5

We'll now follow another series of rolls, where you make continuous $10 pass-line and come bets and take single odds on every number rolled.

Come-out roll	5 (point)	$10 and $10 odds
First come roll	6	$10 and $10 odds
Second come roll	8	$10 and $10 odds
Third come roll	11	$10 win on come roll
Fourth come roll	9	$10 and $10 odds
Next roll	6	$22 win on repeat of 6 as a come bet. $10 and $10 odds

At this point, we'll pause and analyze your position. You have already won $32 on your come bets: $10 for the 11, which is a winner on the come bet as it is on the pass-line, and $22 on the 6 as a repeating come bet. The $22 payoff was $10 for the come bet, and $12 for the odds bet at 6-5 or $12-$10.

You now have the following come bets working: 6, 8 and 9, in addition to your pass-line bet on the 5. The 6 is still working as a come bet because you had placed $10 in the come box prior to the 6 repeating, and thus it was an "off and on" bet. I'll explain this.

When the 6 repeated, the dealer, if he was working in Las Vegas, would merely pay you $22, and announce the bet was "off and on," leaving the come bet with odds in the 6 place number, and also leaving the $10 in the come box. In some of the smaller clubs in Northern Nevada, there would be a more elaborate payoff which, although accomplishing the same end, slows up the game.

There, the dealer would first pay you with $22, for your win. Then the dealer would remove the come bet and the odds from the place number. Next, the dealer would replace the come bet and odds bet in the place number 6, and replace the $10 bet in the come box as the next bet. This tedious method of paying off is done where dealers are inexperienced, or where the casino operators don't trust their skill at payoffs, and so they do the payoff step by step. This need not concern you if you bet in a major casino in northern Nevada, or in practically any casino in Las Vegas. The payoff and the principle are the same, and if a come bet repeats, and you have $10 in the come box, the bet will merely be "off and on," with the come bet still working, and the $10 still in the come box, set for the next roll of the dice.

Let's return to our game. You have three come bets in addition to the point of 5 working, and have $80 on the layout in line, come and odds bets. You have already collected $32 from winning bets.

Next roll	10	$10 and $10 odds
Next roll	9	$25 win as come bet on the 9 $10 and $10 odds
Next roll	5	$25 win as point bet $10 and $10 odds

Again, we'll pause to analyze your position. The 5 was the point and, since it was repeated, there is now a new come-out roll about to begin.

On this new come-out roll, all the come bets will be working; that is, they'll be paid off if any of them repeat, and if a 7 is rolled on the come-out roll, they'll all be losing bets. However, on come-out rolls, all odds bets on come bets are off, which means that, should a 7 be rolled, the odds bets would be returned to you, though you would lose your basic come bets. If any come number repeats on the come-out roll, you will be paid off for your basic come bet, but again, your odds bet on that repeating number will be returned to you. All other numbers and their odds bets would remain intact, however, if a come bet repeats on the come-out roll.

There is no rhyme or reason for this rule, but this is the general rule in all casinos in Nevada and you should be aware of it.

At this moment, before resuming the roll, let's look over the layout and see what bets have been made and what numbers are "working." You have the following come bets out: 5, 6, 8, 9 and 10, all with free odds. There is $100 on the table in bets, but you have already collected $82 in winning bets. The roll continues.

New come-out roll	6 (point)	$10 win as come bet. Odds are returned. You bet $10 and $10 odds on the point
Next roll	12	$10 loss as come bet
Next roll	8	$22 win as come bet repeats $10 and $10 odds
Next roll	10	$30 win as come bet $10 and $10 odds
Next roll	10	$30 win as come bet $10 and $10 odds
Next roll	9	$25 win as come bet $10 and $10 odds
Next roll	3	$10 loss as come bet

Next roll	8	Win $22 as come bet
		$10 and $10 odds
Next roll	5	$25 win as come bet
		$10 and $10 odds
Next roll	11	$10 win as come bet
Next roll	5	$25 win as come bet
		$10 and $10 odds
Final roll	7	$10 win as come bet
		$20 loss as pass-line bet
		$100 loss on all come bets working
The final result of this roll:		Total wins: $291
		Total losses: $140
		Net win $151

In our illustration of this roll, we had you make continuous come bets right to the end. You were putting out a lot of money on the layout, but collecting on practically every roll, at better than even-money, when your numbers repeated. This kind of roll demonstrates why most players bet right, or with the dice. As numbers repeat, they get constant payoffs and these winnings can multiply if you, in addition to your constant bets, continually press or raise your bets as the roll continues.

For purposes of our demonstration, however, I had you making $10 bets and not deviating from these bets. Even so, you won some nice money. Craps can be a very exciting and profitable game if played correctly, taking odds on every bet, and come betting is an integral part of practically every winning strategy.

To summarize the come bet:

It can only be made after the come-out roll. It is identical to the pass-line bet, except in timing. Free odds are permitted on every come bet, but these odds are off on the come-out roll. Come bets, however, are always working.

DON'T COME BETS

```
┌─────────┐
│ Don't   │
│ Come    │
│  Bar    │
│ ▦ ▦     │
└─────────┘
```

Don't come bets are identical to don't pass bets except for timing. Whereas a don't pass bet can only be made on the come-out roll, a don't come bet can be made on any roll after a point is established. The same rules apply to both. If a 2 or 3 is rolled, it's a winning bet for the wrong bettor; if a 12 is rolled, it's a standoff; and if a 7 or 11 is rolled, it's an immediate losing bet for the don't bettor.

Should any other number be rolled, either a 4, 5, 6, 8, 9 or 10, that number, if repeated before a 7 shows on the dice, is a losing bet for the don't bettor. If a 7 is rolled before the number is repeated, then the wrong bettor wins, either as a line or don't come bettor. Therefore, at any craps table, after a point has been established and a few don't come bets have also been established and are in the place box numbers, you can be sure that the wrong bettors are silently praying for the 7 to show on the dice.

Just as with don't pass bets, free odds are allowed to be made by the don't come bettor. And the odds, when made, are *laid* against the point number. Let's review the odds on all point numbers:

Point Number	Odds Against Repeating Before a 7 Is Rolled
4 or 10	2-1
5 or 9	3-2
6 or 8	6-5

The house has the same advantage on don't come bets that it has on don't pass bets—approximately 1.4%. When the don't come bet is made with single odds, the house edge is reduced to 0.8%, and when double odds are permitted, the casino advantage drops still further to 0.6%.

You make a don't come bet by placing chips in the don't come box, after the point is established on the come-out roll. If another number is rolled, for example, a 5, then the chips are removed from the don't come box by the dealer and placed on the top of the place number box 5, as shown in the next illustration:

If you, the wrong bettor, now wish to lay odds against the 5, you hand your bet to the dealer who will place these chips on top of the original don't come bet now resting above the place number box 5. These chips will be put there at a tilt, to show that they're odds bets. If there are too many chips to place on top of the original bet, they will be put alongside the original bet, again showing that these additional chips are odds.

Let's follow a series of rolls to better understand the concept of don't come bets. Again, you are a $10 bettor at a casino that permits only single free odds bets.

Come-out roll	10 (point)	$10 and $20 odds (2-1) don't pass bet
First roll	5	$10 and $15 odds (3-2)
Next roll	7	$10 loss on don't come bet
		$20 win on don't pass bet

$20 win on don't come bet on 5
Total wins: $40
Total losses: $10
                 ————
Net win $30

Let's now follow another series of rolls at the same casino. Each roll after the come-out roll is called a come roll, despite the fact that you are betting don't come. On the come-out roll, you are making a don't pass bet.

Come-out roll	10 (point)	$10 and $20 odds (2-1) don't pass bet
First roll	5	$10 and $15 odds (3-2)
Second come roll	4	$10 and $20 odds (2-1)
Next come roll	6	$10 and $12 odds (6-5)
Next roll	9	$25 loss on the don't pass bet $10 and $15 odds (3-2)

Let's pause and review the situation. At this moment, there is a new come-out roll since the point of 9 was repeated. You now have three don't come numbers working; the 4, 6 and 9. You have $30 in don't come bets and $47 in odds bets on the table, for a total of $77, and have already lost $25.

On a come-out roll, not only are the don't come bets working, just as come bets, *but the odds bets on don't come bets are working as well*. Again, this is a peculiarity of casinos without any apparent reason. Therefore, a 7 rolled on the come-out not only wins all the don't come bets for you, but your odds bet win as well. So, at this moment, you, the wrong bettor, are praying for a 7. And your prayers are rewarded.

New come-out roll   7 $10 loss on don't pass bet
                                  $60 win on all don't come bets
                                  with odds

Total wins:	$60
Total losses:	$35
Net win:	$25

Don't come bets, along with their free odds, are always working, even on the come-out rolls. If the new come-out roll in our theoretical series had been a 4 instead of a 7, you would have lost $30 on your don't come bet and odds on the 4 previously established.

This vulnerability to repeats is why most players bet with the dice rather than against them. The wrong bettor is laying odds, putting out more money on the layout than he will collect if he wins the bet. With a few repeats, he may lose heart and money.

This is not to say that don't come bets are poor bets—they certainly are as valid as come bets—but it takes a strong personality to bet them. Not all players can be wrong bettors, for they don't want to be in a situation where every roll of the dice can wipe out another number and all the money they have on that number.

On the other hand, unlike come bets, a 7 on the dice wins all previously established don't come bets, while a 7 loses all previously established come bets. And, the wrong bettor, betting don't come, can be hit one number at a time, while the right bettor, betting come bets, can be wiped out by one number—the 7.

There's another difference between come and don't come bets, already mentioned during the roll. The come bets are always working, even on the come-out roll, but their underlying odds are off on the come-out roll, so, if a 7 is rolled on the come-out roll, the come bettor loses all his come bets, but his odds are returned to him without loss.

Not many players know that all don't pass and don't come bets can be removed at the option of the player at any time in practically all casinos. The reason is simple. Since a 7 can be rolled in six ways, and any point number in fewer ways, the don't bettor has an advantage over the house on every don't pass and don't come bet *where a number has already been established*. Therefore, the house will permit these bets to be taken down by the player. But again, this should never be done. Why should a bettor relinquish his advantage?

To summarize the don't come bet:

1. It can be made at any time after the come-out roll where a point has been established.

2. It is subject to the same rules as a don't pass bet. If a 2 or 3 is rolled, it's an immediate winner. A 12 is a standoff, and a 7 or 11 an immediate loser.

3. If any other number is rolled, either a 4, 5, 6, 8, 9 or 10, if that number is repeated before a 7 shows, the don't come bettor loses his bet. If a 7 is rolled before the number is repeated, the don't come bettor wins.

4. A don't come bet, along with the odds, is always working.

7

The Place Bets

This is one of the most popular of the betting areas for right bettors, who want the dice to show a series of repeating place numbers. The place betting area consists of all the point numbers, 4, 5, 6, 8, 9 and 10 and looks like this on the layout.

This betting area is directly in front of each of the standing dealers, within easy reach, for not only are all place bets put in the appropriate spaces by the dealer but the center of each place box number is used for come bets that have been established. The smaller box area above the top "place bets" is used for don't come bets.

When you bet on one or more of the place numbers, you are betting that the number will repeat before a 7 is thrown. To make this bet, you must give the dealer the proper number of chips, and tell the dealer exactly which number or numbers you want to bet. You may bet on only one or all of them, or on any group of numbers. If you desire to bet on only one, for example, the 5, you will give the dealer your chips and say "Put it on the 5," or "Cover the 5," or "Give me the 5." The dealer will then place the chips in the area designated as "place bets," either below or above the box number 5.

Some players only make place bets on the "outside numbers," the 4, 5, 9 and 10. Others will only bet the 6 and 8 as place numbers because of the lower house edge of 1.52%. And many place number bettors spread their bets "across the board," covering all numbers not originally covered by the pass-line bet.

If you wish to bet place numbers, you should bet them in denominations of $5 or multiples thereof on the 4, 5, 9 and 10, and denominations and multiples of $6 on the 6 and 8. This is to ensure the correct payoffs. The following are the payoffs made on these numbers, and the house edge on each number.

Place Number	Payoff	House Edge
4	9-5	6.67%
5	7-5	4.0%
6	7-6	1.52%
8	7-6	1.52%
9	7-5	4.0%
10	9-5	6.67%

We can readily see that the house edge on all these place bets is much higher than the advantage the casino enjoys on line and come bets, especially with free odds. You can't take or lay free odds with place bets; you get only the odds listed above, for they are standard in all American casinos. The house advantage is high because the payoffs are below the correct ones that should be made.

The correct payoff on a 4 or 10 should be 2-1; on the 5 or 9, 3-2 (7½-5); and on the 6 or 8, 6-5.

Place bets may be made at any time after the come-out roll. They are "off" and not working on the come-out. They may be made in any amounts up to the house limit, which is usually $500 on the 4, 5, 9 and 10, and $600 on the 6 and 8. These place bets may also be taken off at any time, without penalty. And, they may be reduced or added to at any time, up to the casino limit.

A place bet differs from a come bet in several major respects:

1. All place bets are off on the come-out roll; thus, they don't lose to a 7 rolled on the come-out, as come bets do.

2. No odds bets may be added, for place bets are paid off at rigid odds.

3. A come bet must first be established, then repeated, for there to be a payoff. A place bet may be made immediately after the come-out roll, and anytime a number comes up on the dice, there is an immediate payoff.

4. Place bets may be added to or reduced at any time by the player, whereas come bets, once made, are established only in the amount of the original bet.

5. Place bets may be declared "off" for one or more rolls at the option of the player, whereas come bets are never off on any roll, and cannot be declared off at the request of the player.

6. The house advantage on place bets is greater than on come bets, with or without free odds.

7. Place bets, to be effective, must be made in minimum amounts of $5 on the 4, 5, 9 or 10, and $6 on the 6 and 8, since all payoffs on the above numbers are made to those amounts. For example, the payoff on a 4 is 9-5, while on a 6 it is 7-6. Come bets may be made for lesser amounts and not necessarily in multiples of $5 or $6.

In some of the downtown casinos in Las Vegas and in other casinos around Nevada where 25¢ bets are permitted, there may be bets allowed of $2.50 on place bets of 4, 5, 9 and 10, and $3 on the 6 and 8. In some casinos, place bettors may bet in even smaller amounts, but for our discussion, we'll deal with a casino allowing minimum amounts of either $5 or $6 only.

If you observe any busy craps table filled with right bettors, there will be much activity involving the place bet numbers. After a point is established, a ton of money will be put on the place number bets, especially on the Las Vegas Strip. Most right bettors, after betting the pass-line, will cover one or more of the place numbers. Several will cover them all, except for the number established on the point.

A gambler, if he has made a pass-line bet, will usually avoid betting on the place number which is also the point established. It is a superfluous bet which gives the house a greater advantage over the player than it has on the pass-line bet.

For example, if you had bet $10 on the pass-line, and the point was 5, and you made a $10 free odds bet as well on the point, the house has a 0.8% advantage on that bet. If you now put an additional $10 in the 5 box as a place number bet, you'll be giving the house a 4.0% advantage on the same number. But some players, when they are on a hot roll, or taking advantage of one, will make place bets on the point, because they want to get as much money as possible on the table. I never recommend covering any place number that has been established as a point.

Let's follow a roll as you make pass-line and place bets at a casino that only permits single odds, to fully understand how these bets are made and paid off. A shooter is coming out, and the roll begins.

Come-out roll	8 (point)	$10 and $10 odds on pass-line bet. $52 bet on place numbers. $12 on the 6, and $10 each on 4, 5, 9 and 10
First come roll	6	$14 win (7-6)
Second roll	9	$14 win (7-5)
Third roll	10	$18 win (9-5)
Next roll	5	$14 win (7-5)
Final roll	7	$52 loss on place bets

$20 loss on pass-line and odds
Total wins: $60
Total losses: $72
                 ⎯⎯⎯⎯
Net loss $12

This roll points out the difficulty with place bets. You need a whole series of repeating numbers in order to make a profit from your original investment if you bet all the place numbers. If a 7 comes up on the first come roll, all your bets are immediately wiped out and lost, which would be an immediate loss of $52 plus your pass-line bet in this example.

It takes at least five repeating numbers for a pass-line bettor covering all place numbers to show a slight profit of about $2. Less than five rolls (assuming the pass-line number hasn't repeated) and he's a loser. If you only bet place numbers, covering all six of them after the come-out roll, and don't bother to bet pass-line, you still must have five numbers rolled in order to make any money.

The habitual place number bettor, if he covers all the numbers time and time again in this manner, whether or not he bets pass-line, loses money in the long run because he's giving the house too big an advantage. The casino has as much as 6.67% on the 4 and 10, 4% on the 5 and 9. Only the 6 and 8 give the house a relatively small advantage of 1.52%.

These high advantages by the house inevitably wipe out the place bettor, grinding him out slowly but surely, and sometimes, at a cold table, with a series of 7s coming out on the dice right after the point has been established, destroying him quickly.

Of all bettors at the craps table, the place bettor who covers all the numbers is most vulnerable to the 7 being thrown. Not only does he lose his pass-line bet, but all his place bets as well—without a single collection. In this respect, the come bettor has a decided advantage because, if a 7 is rolled right after a point has been established, the come bettor will lose his pass-line and odds bet just as the place bettor will, but the first bet in the come box is a winner for the come bettor. The difference is considerable. If both players were $10 bettors, the place bettor would lose a total of $72, while the come bettor would lose a total of $10. In the long run, this difference is potent. The come bettor, by betting intelligently, will survive much longer at a cold table than will a place bettor; thus, when the hot roll finally comes around, the come bettor might very well be there to take advantage of it, while the place bettor will have left the table long before, tapped out.

Should there be any reason, then, for making place number bets? Yes. It would be better to limit them to the 6 and 8 for the most part, since these numbers might not come up as come numbers and you might want to have them covered for they are the heart of any hot roll. Sometimes, in the middle of a fiery hot roll, when numbers are continually repeating, you might want to cover the 5 and 9 also, without waiting to re-establish these numbers with come bets. The 5, 6, 8 and 9 are known as inside numbers. They are the only worthwhile numbers to bet as place bets. If possible, only the 6 and 8 should be bet as place bets, but examine the winning strategies and "A Dice Story" in this book to see what methods may be employed effectively when betting place numbers.

To reiterate, never make indiscriminate place number bets, betting across the board. This is done by players who inevitably are big losers. These foolish bettors are the delight of casinos because they give the house such a big edge on these bets. If all bettors limited their wagers to pass-line with free odds, come bets with free odds, the casinos might very well close up their craps tables.

But the numbers are there, tempting the greedy player. He knows if any come up, he'll get an immediate payoff, and this temptation is too great for many players, overcoming their ability to think clearly in terms of house odds and casino advantage.

BUYING THE 4 AND 10

There is one way to lower the 6.67% advantage on the 4 and 10 place bets, and that's by buying them. You do this by giving the house a 5% commission, and announcing that you will buy them.

If bought instead of placed, the 4 and 10 will pay the correct 2-1 if rolled, instead of the 9-5 the casino pays off on the place bets. By buying the 4 and/or 10, the house advantage drops to 4.76%, which is considerably greater than the other place numbers and much higher than getting these numbers as come or pass-line bets at 0.8%.

After a 4 or 10 is bought, a small "buy" button is put atop the chips in the place bet number, to show that they are not ordinary place bets.

LAYING BETS

Not only can you buy bets, but you can lay bets as well. Some wrong players lay the odds against a place point appearing on the dice. In essence, they're betting wrong and laying bets in the same way that right bettors are placing or buying them.

This is done rarely, but a wrong bettor may lay bets against any of the place points, 4, 5, 6, 8, 9 or 10. To do this, you pay a 5% commission which is not based on the wager, but on the payoff. For example, if you lay $40 against the 10, you pay $1 or 5% of the potential winning bet of $20, since you are laying the bet at 2-1.

The casino advantage on the lay bets is as follows: On the 4 and 10, it's 2.44%; on the 5 and 9, it's 3.23%, and on the 6 and 8, it's a high 4%.

The bet is made by telling the dealer you want to bet against the numbers and an immediate commission is paid to the house. A "buy" button is placed on the bet, which is moved to the same area as don't come bets.

If a 7 comes up and you win your bet, if you are a lay bettor, you must pay an additional 5% commission if you want your bets to stand. If a lay wager has been made, and you decide to take it off before it wins or loses, the commission will also be returned to you. These bets may be removed at any time, and while they stand, they're always working.

8

Field, Big 6 and Big 8, and Proposition Bets

FIELD BETS

This betting space covers a large area of the layout—an inordinate amount of space, in my opinion, because the Field Bet gets very little play from astute gamblers. It does have an attraction for beginners and certain systems players, but they'd be better off trying their systems on the pass-line where the odds are much better.

The Field Bet looks like this on a typical craps layout in Atlantic City and on the Strip in Las Vegas.

The Field Bet is slightly different in the downtown Las Vegas casinos, where the 12 is paid off at 3-1, and in the Northern Nevada houses where, in some casinos, the 2 is paid off at 3-1. Where the payoffs on the 2 and 12 are both 2-1, the house advantage on this bet is 5.55%. Where either the 2 or 12 is paid off at 3-1, the house edge drops to 2.77%.

To make a Field Bet, you put your chips in the Field Bet betting area. You may wager from as little as the house minimum all the way up to a bet equal to the house maximum. The bet, if won, is paid off at even-money, except for the 2 and 12. If any of the numbers appearing on the betting space are thrown on the very next roll, you win your bet. If any of the numbers missing on the Field Bet are rolled (5, 6, 7 or 8), the bet is lost.

Field Bets are therefore one-roll bets, dependent upon the very next roll of the dice. They are then paid off or lost immediately. The bet may be made at any time, even on the come-out roll, for, as one-roll bets, they're always working and never off.

At first glance, it appears that the bet favors the player, since there are so many numbers listed for the bettor, and two of them are paid off at 2-1. However, the numbers that aren't displayed, though few in number, have more ways of being rolled by the dice than the numbers shown.

Let's examine the mathematics of this bet and see how the casino edge is determined. I'll list the numbers that pay off on this bet, and the chances of rolling each of these numbers.

Number	Combinations	Ways to Make
2	(1-1) × 2 (pays 2-1)	2
3	(1-2, 2-1)	2
4	(1-3, 3-1, 2-2)	3
9	(3-6, 6-3, 4-5, 5-4)	4
10	(4-6, 6-4, 5-5)	3
11	(5-6, 6-5)	2
12	(6-6) × 2 (pays 2-1)	2
	Total ways to win	18

There are 20 ways to make the missing numbers, 5, 6, 7 and 8, however, and therefore the player has a disadvantage of 5.55% on this bet. When the house permits a 3-1 payoff, either on the 2 or 12, the player disadvantage drops to 2.77%.

Field Bets should not be made if you want to win at craps, since there are much better wagers to be made on the layout, such as pass-line and come bets. Even though the field bettors don't have the anxiety of waiting for a point to be repeated—whereas those other bets involve a delay till the result is known—they pay for this by getting poor odds for their money.

BIG 6 AND BIG 8 BETS

These bets aren't as prominently displayed as the Field Bets, but are almost as big as the don't come box. The Big 6 and Big 8 wagers get some action and you can be sure, when seeing a player make these bets, that he or she is completely ignorant of the game of craps because this bet should never be made under any circumstances.

The bet is simple enough and can be made at any time—even on the come-out roll. It's always working. You make this bet by placing chips in either the Big 6 or Big 8 box or both, if you wish. You may bet the house minimum all the way up to the house maximum. You are betting that the number you have bet on, either 6 or 8, or both, will repeat before a 7 shows on the dice. If it doesn't repeat, and a 7 is rolled, you lose your bet. If the number 6 or 8 (whatever you bet on) repeats before the 7 is rolled, you win your bet.

The trouble with this bet is that it is paid at even-money, and

therefore you give the house a huge edge. Since there are six ways
to roll a 7, and only five to roll either a 6 or 8, the odds against the
bet winning is 6-5, which boils down to a 9.09% advantage for the
house.

If you like the 6 and 8, you'd be much better off betting them
as place numbers, by wagering $6 in the place number box on the
appropriate number. You'd be paid off at 7-6 on this bet, and the
house would only have a 1.52% edge.

But people keep making the Big 6 and Big 8 bets, and keep
losing in the long run.

No player can be expected to buck a 9.09% disadvantage and
still end up a winner. This bet should always be avoided, with one
exception. The casino operated by Resorts International at Atlantic
City pays off Big 6 and Big 8 wagers at 7-6, not even-money, paying
the same odds as a 6 or 8 place bet.

PROPOSITION BETS

We now come to the center of the layout, which is under the
control of the stickman. There are several bets displayed here,
none of which are worthwhile. Nonetheless, I'll cover them one at
a time and examine them more fully to explain why they have no
value for the astute craps player.

The center is divided into two types of bets—the Hardways
and the one roll bets. I'll first discuss the one-roll bets, beginning
with the Any Seven Bet.

Any Seven
This is a one-roll bet that pays off at 4-1. This bet gets perhaps
the least action of any on the layout because even the most dense
and ignorant bettors know that it is a terrible bet to make. The
correct odds are 5-1, and the 4-1 payoff means the house has an
advantage of 16.67% on this wager.

On some layouts, the listed payoff is "5 for 1." Since you may

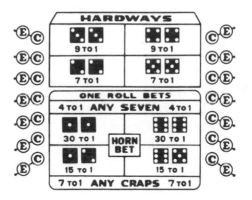

encounter this term at many casinos, it's a good time to discuss the word "for" in terms of payoffs, because it may not be fully understood, and is a trap for the unwary bettor.

When a payoff is set at 5-1, you, the winner, receive $5 plus your original bet of $1, for a total of $6. When a payoff is at 5 for 1, you receive $5, and that *includes your $1 bet*, for a total of $5. That's $1 less than the 5-1 payoff. When the word "for" is on the layout, the payoff is exactly one level lower than stated. 5 for 1 means 4-1, and 30 for 1 means 29-1, because the $1 bet that you made is not separately returned to you along with your winning bet.

To make an Any Seven bet, you can either give your chips to the standing dealer and inform him that you wish to bet on the Seven, or you can throw your chip or chips to the stickman and tell him to make the bet for you. It's a one-roll bet; therefore, the very next roll of the dice determines the outcome, even on the come-out roll. The bet is always working and never off. If a 7 is thrown on the next roll of the dice, the Any Seven bet wins at 4-1. If any other number is thrown, then the bet is a losing one.

Since a 7 can only be made six ways, and there are thirty-six possible combinations on the dice, the chances of a 7 appearing on the next roll is six in thirty-six, or 5-1 against. The payoff on this bet is 4-1; and the house has an edge of 16.67% on the wager. Needless to say, this bet should never be made.

Any Craps

This bet is usually at the bottom of the proposition bet layout, and is paid off at 7-1, and in many casinos at 8 for 1, which is the same thing. This is another one-roll bet and is always working. If you make this bet and the next roll of the dice comes up "craps," that is, either a 2, 3 or 12, you win your bet at 7-1. If any other number comes up on the dice, you lose your bet.

Since there are only four ways to make craps and there are thirty-six possible combinations of the dice, the chances of rolling a craps on any one roll are four in thirty-six. Therefore, the odds are 8-1 against the Any Craps bet. The payoff is at 7-1, for a house advantage of 11.1%. This bet should never be made.

Betting the 2, 3, 11 and 12

These are all one-roll bets which win or lose depending on the next roll of the dice, and all can be bet individually on the center layout.

The 2 and the 12 can only be rolled one way, and therefore the odds against either of these numbers coming up on the next throw of the dice is 35-1. The payoff ranges from 30-1 in some casinos down to 30 for 1, or 29-1 in others. When the odds are paid off at 30-1, the house edge is 13.89%. When it's paid off at 29-1, the casino advantage is an horrendous 16.67%.

The 3 or 11 can be rolled only two ways each, and the odds should be 17-1, but they're paid off at 15-1 or 15 for 1, giving the house a 16.67% edge when paid off at 15 for 1 (14-1). When paid off at 15-1 in the "liberal" casinos, the casino advantage drops to 11.1%.

Despite this terrible house edge, the 11 is one of the most popular bets on the center layout. This bet, along with Any Craps, gets a lot of play, particularly on the come-out roll. Needless to say, the house loves action on these bets, but any player betting them is a downright sucker.

Horn Bets

This is a popular bet in both Atlantic City and in the northern Nevada casinos, but gets relatively little play on the Strip in Las Vegas. By making this bet, you are covering individually the 2, 3, 11 and 12, all with one bet. You must therefore bet at least four units, or four chips, to make the bet, and should any of those numbers show on the next roll of the dice, you win according to the usual casino payoff, but the casino retains the three remaining losing chips.

This bet allows you to make four bad bets at once, and it should never be made.

There are still other bets that can be made, other than the usual ones on the center layout such as Hop Bets, betting that a particular number will show next on the dice. All of these have terrible disadvantages to you and should never be made. The best advice I can give is to stay away from any proposition and one-roll bets in the center. They're only for fools.

Hardway Bets

A point number is said to be a "hardway," when it's rolled as a pair, with the same dots showing on each die. For example, a four is a hardway when rolled 2-2; a six when rolled 3-3; an eight when rolled 4-4, and a 10 when rolled 5-5. Each of the hardways can only be rolled one way, with one combination of the dice.

These are not one-roll bets however. Here's how they work. If you bet on a hardway number, for example the hard 4, you're betting that the 4 will come up 2-2, or hard, before it comes up "easy" as 1-3, or 3-1, or before a 7 shows on the dice.

Since there is only one way to make any hardway number, and since there are six ways to make a 7, and two easy ways to make a 4, the odds against a hard 4 are 8-1. The house pays off at 7-1, giving itself an advantage over you of 11.1%.

The hard 10 (5-5) can only be rolled one way, and there are two easy ways to roll it, and six ways to roll the 7, and the same odds and house advantage prevail on this number as on the hard 4, a whopping 11.1%.

The hard six (3-3) and the hard eight (4-4) can each be made only one way hard, but four ways easy. Counting the six ways a 7 can be rolled, the odds against either of these being rolled is 10-1. The house only pays 9-1 on the hard 6 or hard 8, and enjoys a 9.09% advantage on these bets.

We've finally come to the end of a series of unsatisfactory and disadvantageous bets for the player on the center layout. None of them should be made—they're all bad. The astute player should avoid getting greedy, trying to win a lot of money for a small bet, and stay away from the center layout, period. It's the best advice I can give you on these bets.

9

Complete Tables of
Odds on All Bets

Bet	Casino Payoff	Casino Advantage
Pass-Line	Even-money	1.41%
With Single Odds	Even-money plus odds	0.8%
With Double Odds	Even-money plus odds	0.6%
Come	Even-money	1.41%
With Single Odds	Even-money plus odds	0.8%
With Double Odds	Even-money plus odds	0.6%
Don't Pass	Even-money	1.4%
With Single Odds	Even-money plus odds	0.8%
With Double Odds	Even-money plus odds	0.6%
Don't Come	Even-money	1.4%
With Single Odds	Even-money plus odds	0.8%
With Double Odds	Even-money plus odds	0.6%
Place Numbers		
4 or 10	9-5	6.67%

Bet	*Casino Payoff*	*Casino Advantage*
4 or 10 (bought)	2-1 (−5% commission)	4.76%
5 or 9	7-5	4%
6 or 8	7-6	1.52%
Big Six and Big Eight	Even-money	9.09%
Field		
With 2 and 12 paying 2-1	Even-money except for 2 and 12	5.55%
With 2 or 12 paying 3-1	Even-money except for 2 and 12	2.77%

Proposition Bets

Bet	*True Odds*	*Casino Payoff*	*House Advantage*
Any 7	5-1	4-1	16.67%
Any Craps	8-1	7-1	11.1%
2	35-1	30-1	13.89%
		29-1	16.67%
3	17-1	15-1	11.1%
		14-1	16.67%
11	17-1	15-1	11.1%
		14-1	16.67%
12	35-1	30-1	13.89%
		29-1	16.67%
Hardways			
4 or 10	8-1	7-1	11.1%
6 or 8	10-1	9-1	9.09%

10

Basic Winning
Strategies

INTRODUCTION

In choosing our basic winning strategies, we must take several factors into consideration. First of all, in order to beat the house at casino craps, you must understand which bets are best for you and avoid making foolish or unprofitable wagers.

In previous chapters, we've gone over all the possible bets available to the gambler on the craps layout and I've emphasized that the line bets with free odds as well as the come and don't come bets, also with free odds, give the house the smallest advantage over the player, less than 1%. It is on these bets I'll concentrate when presenting winning strategies.

Besides knowing what bets to make, you should also know exactly how many bets to make in succession and how much money to have out on the layout at any one time. If you have too many bets working, a short losing streak will wipe out your bankroll in no time at all. If you don't have enough wagers on the layout, you won't be able to take advantage of a "hot roll" and thus will miss an opportunity to make a lot of money from one roll. My betting strategies will permit you to conserve your bankroll while allowing for the possibility of maximizing your profits.

You must also have an adequate bankroll when using these strategies. If your bankroll is too small, you'll find yourself unable to take advantage of favorable situations, and will, in effect, be playing with "scared money." Scared money is inadequate funds and forces you either to hedge your bet when you should be bold, or worse, causes you to make foolish bets in the hope of winning a lot of money on relatively small wagers. To do this, you must make center proposition wagers which give the casino its greatest edge over you. Therefore, an adequate bankroll is of prime importance.

Finally, you must know when to leave the table, either as a winner or loser. If you lose too much money at any one session of play, you might negate your chances of ever recouping your losses at another gambling session. And, if winning, you must leave so that you retain some of your winnings. The old adage states that the gambler should limit his losses and let his winnings ride. I add to this *that to be a winner, the gambler must leave the table as a winner*.

If we put all these factors together, we can work out a winning strategy and beat the casino. Let's now summarize these points.

1. We must make only those bets which give the house a minimal advantage.

2. We must make enough bets to take advantage of a hot roll. At the same time, we don't want too much money out on the layout in relation to our bankroll, so that one poor roll hurts us too badly.

3. We must have a sufficient bankroll to weather temporary losses and to prevent us from making foolish bets.

4. We must know when to leave the table, limiting our losses, and if we have been winning, to leave as a winner.

In discussing our basic winning strategies, I'll cover those for both right and wrong bettors, but, since right bettors constitute the vast majority of players, I'll start with a method of beating the casino by betting right, or with the dice.

BETTING WITH THE DICE—THE RIGHT BETTOR'S
BASIC WINNING STRATEGY

The bets I'm going to outline will be limited to pass-line and come bets, both with free odds. When you make single odds bets, the house advantage is no more than 0.8%, and if the casino permits double odds bets, it drops down to 0.6%. We're going to drop the house advantage even lower, because I'm going to give you a few tips on how to continually take advantage of these bets for your benefit and the detriment of the house.

In discussing our money bets, at times I'm going to use units and at other times actual money figures. Therefore, whether you intend to bet $1 or $500, you can take full advantage of these strategies. For instance, if I suggest betting 3 units on the pass-line, the $1 bettor will bet $3, the $5 bettor $15, the $25 bettor $75, and the $100 gambler will wager $300, but no matter what will be bet, the same principles will apply.

For our first basic strategy, 3 units will be wagered if the house only offers single odds, and 2 units will be wagered if double odds are permitted. These unit bets will be made on both the pass-line and come bets.

This difference in unit betting is not arbitrary but made for a definite reason—to benefit you. When only single odds are allowed, if the point is 6 or 8, you will be permitted to make as much as a 5 unit bet behind the line as an odds bet, rather than a standard 3 unit bet as a free odds wager. If the point is 5 or 9, you can bet 4 units behind the line as a free odds bet. These enhanced odds bets are definitely to your advantage.

If double odds are permitted, our bet is 2 units on both the pass-line and come bets, because, if the point is a 6 or 8, we can then make a 5 unit bet on these numbers as free odds wagers. On all other numbered points, we can bet double the original line or come bet.

Not many players are aware of this chance to put more money behind the line when betting in these units, or multiples thereof, but it's permitted in practically all American casinos. For example, where double odds are permitted, if you have 4 units on the pass-line and the point is 6, you may now bet 10 units as your free odds bet. If a few points are repeated, you can really hurt the casino.

After the pass-line bet is made, you will then make two come bets, or enough come bets so that two numbers are established as your come bet numbers. If you have been betting 3 units on the pass-line, you'll continue with 3 unit bets in the come box. And if you've been making 2 unit wagers, you'll go on with those same 2 unit bets. On all bets, you'll take the maximum free odds offered.

After you have a pass-line bet with a point established, and two come numbers established, you stop betting until either your pass-line bet wins, a come bet is repeated, or a 7 shows on the dice.

To illustrate this strategy more clearly, we'll use money units of $5 and follow a sample roll of the dice at a casino that allows single odds only.

Come-out roll	6 (point)	$15 and $25 odds
First come roll	9	$15 and $20 odds
Second come roll	4	$15 and $15 odds

If we had been at a casino that permitted double odds, the same roll would look like this in terms of bets:

Come-out roll	6 (point)	$10 and $25 odds
First come roll	9	$10 and $20 odds
Second come roll	4	$10 and $20 odds

We stop our betting now in either casino because we don't want to put too much money out on the table at any one time. If a 7 now shows on the dice, we will lose all our bets, and we're most vulnerable at this moment, but in the long run we won't get too hurt because we're never giving the house more than 0.8% on our bets. And we have three numbers working for us betting this way, which gives us a very good chance of repeat numbers and wins.

This method is about the best one you, as a right player, can use for your basic strategy. It gives you the opportunity of winning a great deal of money during a hot roll, and allows you to spend a long time at the table, weathering small losing streaks, until that one hot roll comes along.

I've observed hundreds of games of craps in my time, and interviewed dozens of casino employees, from dealers all the way up to casino managers. They agree that the bettor who uses this strategy is a "tough player," one who gives the house the most trouble, because his losses are generally low and his winnings can really burn a casino.

Let's go back to our sample roll at a casino that offers single odds, return to the beginning, and then follow the roll to its end.

Come-out roll	6 (point)	$15 and $25 odds
First come roll	9	$15 and $20 odds
Second come roll	4	$15 and $15 odds
Next come roll	5	It doesn't affect our bets
Next roll	4	$45 win on come bet of 4. Since our come bet is returned to us, we make another $15 come bet, to keep two come bets working
Next roll	5	$15 and $20 odds
Next roll	9	$45 win on come bet of 9. We make another come bet of $15
Next roll	11	Win $15
Next roll	8	$15 and $25 odds

Let's pause at this moment. We now have a $15 bet and $25 odds on the pass-line number 6, and two come bets, one on the 5 of $15 and $20 odds and another on the 8 of $15 and $25 odds. We've already won $105 on this roll, and have three numbers working.

Next roll	12	It doesn't affect our bets
Next roll	11	It doesn't affect our bets

Next roll	8	$45 win on come bet of 8. We make another come bet of $15
Next roll	7	$15 win as come bet
		$40 loss on pass-line
		$35 loss on come bet on 5

Total wins:	$165
Total losses:	$75
Net win	$90

To summarize our basic winning strategy for Right Bettors:

1. We bet 3 units on the pass-line with single odds, or 2 units with double odds.

2. We make two come bets of 3 units each with single odds, or two come bets of 2 units each with double odds.

3. We always take the maximum odds permitted, and take advantage of extra odds on the 6 and 8 with both single and double odds bets, and the 5 and 9 with single odds bets.

4. After our three numbers are established, we stop betting. If a come bet is repeated, we make still another come bet, because we always want two of them working for us.

5. If the pass-line point is made, we make an identical pass-line bet of either 3 units with single odds, or 2 units with double odds.

That's the basic strategy that will brand the right bettor as a "tough player," for the house is given a minimum edge, in this situation.

Bankroll and Money Management

Our betting method calls for a complete cycle of bets: one pass-line and two come bets, all with free odds. The method illustrated in our sample roll called for about 20 betting units on any one cycle. To allow yourself a sufficient reserve, you should have between 140 and 200 units, or between 7 and 10 times a complete cycle of betting units.

This will be our ratio no matter what we bet. If you're a $1 bettor you should have from $140 to $200. For your bankroll, simply count the units bet in one cycle, multiply by 7 for the minimum, and by 10 for the maximum.

If you are a $15 bettor, you would have between $700 and $1,000 in the rails before making a single bet, in order to have enough reserves to withstand temporary losses at the table. Betting right, or with the dice, can mean many small losses while waiting for that hot roll and the big win. Make certain you have enough to play with so that you'll be around when the hot roll comes.

When to Leave the Table

Many players don't really know when to leave the table, and this uncertainty dooms many of them to losses after they've had some good runs at the table. If they're winning, they inevitably lose all they've won, dig in their pockets for more money, and then lose that as well. To prevent this, I'm going to give you a valuable piece of advice that you should always follow when playing craps.

Don't expect more than one hot roll per session of play. After that roll is over, leave the table.

What's a hot roll? It can't be exactly defined, but anytime the shooter has made three or four points, anytime there's been a series of ten to fifteen numbers repeating on the dice, anytime a shoot takes at least twenty minutes to complete, you've had a hot roll going. After that hot hand is over, take the money and run.

What if there hasn't been a hot roll, but the dice have been passing steadily? Then, if you've won at least 50-60 betting units, prepare to leave as a winner. Play out another complete cycle of betting. If that cycle earns you more money, stay around and keep playing. But if that last cycle loses you money, get away with some winnings intact.

Always try and leave a winner, if possible. If you're winning, and give it all back, you're not a winner. When you have the casino's money in your pocket after leaving the table, you can start another session at a craps table with their money, and feel loose and easy.

This is not to say that you must always put a limit on your winnings, but in craps money is often on the table in large amounts before you're able to make any collection at all. You must temper your wins with this fact—a few bad rolls and all your winnings can evaporate.

If you're losing, set a limit also. Never lose more than you've brought to the table. Never! If you find that you don't have enough in the rails to cover another complete cycle of bets, leave the table. Otherwise you'll be reaching into your pocket and, if you do this a few times at one table, you might be completely tapped out.

It's not always possible to win at a craps table, but that doesn't mean that one bad session should ruin or destroy you. You should always have a reserve for another session in which your luck might be much better.

I believe, for serious play, that the units brought to a table should be between $\frac{1}{7}$ and $\frac{1}{10}$ of the total reserve for gambling. You should never lose more than that $\frac{1}{7}$ or $\frac{1}{10}$ at any one session of play.

The better you control your bankroll and manage your money, the more chance you have of coming out a winner. Together with our tough basic strategy, you have the best possibilities of beating the house.

BETTING AGAINST THE DICE—THE WRONG BETTOR'S BASIC WINNING STRATEGY

In formulating a basic winning strategy for the wrong bettor, we are guided by the same principles that were used in our right bettor's strategy. These are:

1. We want to give the house only a minimal advantage on every bet.

2. We want to make a limited number of bets to preserve our

capital and yet enough to take advantage of a favorable roll.

3. We want to have an adequate bankroll.

4. We want to leave the table at an appropriate time, preferably as a winner.

With these concepts in mind, let's examine a solid betting strategy for the wrong bettor. First of all, we'll stick to the line and don't come bets, but instead of taking odds on all bets, we'll be laying odds, giving the house no more than a 0.8% edge.

Your first wager will be a don't pass bet of 1 or 2 betting units. Your minimum bet should be $5 so that you can lay odds on the 6 and 8, at 6-5. If you bet less than that at any casino with a $1 minimum, you won't be able to lay odds on those two numbers. In laying odds, you'll always lay *single* odds, because, although double odds give you a slightly better percentage, namely 0.2%, you want to limit the money you have out. For purposes of this strategy you'll constantly be betting two $5 units, though 1 unit wouldn't make any difference, except in the amount of money out on the table.

After your don't pass bet and the point is established, you make a don't come bet of 2 units, again laying single odds. Then, after your don't come number is established, you make still another don't come bet, so that you have three numbers working, one on don't pass and two on don't come, all with single odds laid against them.

When laying odds, if your basic bet is $10, you'll be laying $20 at 2-1 against the 4 or 10; $15 at 3-2 against the 5 or 9, and $12 on the 6 and 8, at 6-5.

We've limited our bets to three numbers, because one of the dangers of wrong betting is having too many numbers as targets for repeats, which are then losing bets for wrong bettors. At the same time, we want enough bets on the layout to take advantage of a cold roll.

Let's now follow a series of rolls where our bettor is wagering $10 on don't pass and making two don't come bets of $10 each, all with single odds.

Even though we're betting don't come, each roll after the come-out roll is commonly called a come roll, and that's the term we'll use as well.

Come-out roll	4 (point)	$10 and $20 odds (2-1)
First come roll	6	$10 and $12 odds (6-5)
Second come roll	5	$10 and $15 odds (3-2)

At this time, we stop betting, having our three numbers established. If a 7 is now rolled, we'll win all our bets.

The roll continues:		
Next roll	3	It doesn't affect our bets
Next roll	10	It doesn't affect our bets
Next roll	6	$22 loss on don't come bet on 6
		We make another don't come bet
Next roll	8	$10 and $12 odds (6-5)
Final roll	7	$20 win on don't pass bet
		$40 win on don't come bets on 5 and 8
		Total wins: $60
		Total losses: $22
		Net win $38

This is the average kind of roll, because most of the time the point will not be made and there will be a limited number of rolls before a shooter sevens out. In making don't come bets, you have to limit them if a hot roll develops, and you must limit your don't pass bets as well, so that one shooter with a hot hand doesn't tap you out. The principles we'll now summarize will protect you from this.

1. We make a 2 unit don't pass bet and lay the correct single odds against the point.

2. We make two don't come bets, establishing two numbers against which we lay single odds. These don't come bets we bet at 2 units each.

3. If a don't come number repeats, we make only one additional don't come bet, never more. This is to protect ourselves against a hot roll.

4. If the point repeats, we make only one other don't pass bet. If the point again is made, we stop betting and wait until the shooter sevens out.

5. We should bring an adequate bankroll with us, consisting of between 7 and 10 times our full betting cycle. In the strategy above mentioned, with $10 basic bets, we'd bring between $500 and $800 to the table.

6. This bankroll, for serious players, should be between ⅐ and ⅒ of the total bankroll.

7. We never reach into our pockets for more money, and if winning from 50 to 60 units, play out one more cycle. If we lose on that cycle, we leave the table.

When betting wrong, you will experience many small wins before that hot roll comes along. Therefore, you must protect yourself from the hot roll, and leave the table as it progresses. If your don't pass bet and your don't come bets have been wiped out by repeats, and the roll is still going on, you should get away from the table.

When betting in single units of $5, the wrong bettor can lay $9 to $6 when the point or come number is a 5 or 9, since you cannot lay 7½-5 at most tables.

11

Aggressive Winning Strategies

Although it's true that dice have no memory, it has not only been my experience, but that of others as well, that the game runs in cycles or streaks, as it were, and these streaks can last a long time. When the dice are hot, number after number comes up to the delight of the right bettor and the dismay of the gambler betting against the dice.

Conversely, when the table is cold and right players are being destroyed by an endless succession of point, 7, the wrong bettors are shouting with glee at the cold dice. And these cold streaks seem to go on and on.

Aggressive betting strategies are devised to take advantage of streaks so that, when they occur, we can win the most money in the shortest possible time.

Like all events at the craps table, because of the random nature of the dice, neither hot nor cold streaks can be predicted. But when they happen and you are in the middle of a streak, it's time to get loose and do some real gambling to make some real money. How do you know when a hot roll is in progress?

You know because the dice keep coming up numbers, and these numbers seem to repeat endlessly, while points are continually being made. You might not have anticipated the hot roll, but once involved in it, you should make full use of its potential for profits. You can do this following our aggressive strategies.

RIGHT BETTING—AGGRESSIVE BASIC WINNING STRATEGY WITH SINGLE ODDS

Our basic aggressive strategy limits our bets to the pass-line and come box, again giving the house a minimal advantage.

1. We bet 3 units on the pass-line, taking single odds.

2. We make two come bets of 3 units each, also with single odds, to establish two come numbers working for us.

3. If a come number repeats, another come bet is made of 5 units, and we take the maximum single odds offered.

4. If the pass-line point is made, we bet 5 units on the next pass-line bet and take maximum single odds.

5. Our increase in bets on both pass-line and come bets is as follows: 3-5-6-9-12 and increments of 3 units thereafter, all with maximum single odds.

You are a $15 bettor at a casino table with single odds offered during a roll:

Come-out roll	5 (point)	$15 and $20 odds
First come roll	8	$15 and $25 odds
Second come roll	4	$15 and $15 odds
Next come roll	8	$45 win on come bet on 8. You now bet $25 (5 units) in come box

Next come roll	5	$45 win on pass-line
		$25 and $30 odds on 5 as come bet
New come-out roll	6	$25 and $25 odds

At this time, we'll pause and look over the table. You have $25 pass-line and $25 odds on the point 6; $15 come and $15 odds on the come bet 4, and $25 come and $30 odds on the 5, for a total of $135. You've already won $90.

Next come roll	12	No effect on your bets
Next come roll	11	No effect on your bets
Next come roll	4	$45 win on the come bet 4
		$25 come bet is made
Next come roll	10	$25 and $25 odds
Next come roll	5	$70 win on the come bet 5
		$30 come bet is placed in come box
Next come roll	6	$55 win on pass-line bet
		$30 come and $50 odds
New come-out roll	9	$30 and $30 odds on point 9

Let's pause once more. When the 4 was repeated, you went up to 5 units only because that bet had been made at 3 units. Each individual number is separate and is raised according to its previous wager, so that you may have different amounts bet on different numbers as they repeat.

Next come roll	3	No effect on your bets
Next come roll	6	$90 win on come bet of 6. You place $45 in come box (9 units)
Next come roll	7	$45 win on come bet in box
		$60 loss on pass-line bet

Next come roll $50 loss on come bet on 10
                                  Total wins: $395
                                  Total losses: $110
                                                ────
                                  Net win $285

And this roll was just warming up! Even with this small streak your profits added up readily. Only two points were made and but four come bets repeated, yet your winnings were considerable.

AGGRESSIVE BASIC WINNING STRATEGY WITH DOUBLE ODDS—RIGHT BETTOR

I would suggest that you go back and look up the basic strategy involved in double odds to familiarize yourself with the method of betting. Our aggressive strategy is as follows:

1. We bet 2 units on the pass-line, and take double odds.

2. We make two come bets of 2 units each, till two come numbers are established, again with double odds.

3. If a come bet repeats, we bet 4 units on our next come bet, taking double odds. We do the same if the pass-line bet is won, by the point repeating. By betting 4 units, we can now take 10 units of free odds on the 6 and 8.

4. As our come and pass-line bets repeat, we keep adding 2 units to our previous underlying bet. We go from 2 to 4 to 6 to 8 and so on, each time taking double odds.

5. We always have two come bets working.

AGGRESSIVE WINNING STRATEGY—WRONG BETTORS

1. We bet 2 units on the don't pass line, laying maximum single odds.

2. We bet 2 units on the two don't come bets, again laying single odds. Then we stop betting.

3. If a don't come number is repeated, we make only one more don't come bet and then stop. If a point is repeated, we make only one more don't pass bet and then stop until the shooter sevens out. This is to prevent a hot roll from ruining us.

4. If a 7 is rolled after the don't pass bet is established, thus making our don't pass bet a winner, we raise our bet from 2 to 3 units on the don't pass line, and again lay single odds.

5. If our don't pass bet is raised to 3 units, then all our subsequent don't come bets will also be 3 units. Don't come bets will always be in the same betting units as the don't pass bet.

6. The key to increasing bets is the don't pass bet. If it is won, our bet is increased, no matter what has happened to the don't come bets.

7. As we continue to win our don't pass bet, we increase our betting units from 2 to 3 to 5 and by 2 units thereafter.

Let's follow a series of rolls to better explain this strategy. You are a $10 bettor at the table.

Come-out roll	5 (point)	$10 and $15 odds (3-2)
First come roll	6	$10 and $12 odds (6-5)
Second come roll	8	$10 and $12 odds (6-5)
Next come roll	9	No effect on your bets
Next come roll	12	No effect on your bets
Next come roll	6	$22 loss on don't come bet on 6. You make another $10 don't come bet.
Next come roll	4	$10 and $20 odds (2-1)
Next come roll	7	$20 win on don't pass-line bet $40 win on don't come bets
New shooter coming out		
New come-out roll	10	$15 (3 units) and $30 odds (2-1)
First come roll	9	$15 and $24 odds (3-2)

Second come roll	7	$15 loss on don't come bet
		$30 win on don't pass bet
		$31 win on don't come bet on 9
New shooter coming out		
New come-out roll	6 (point)	$25 (5 units) and $30 odds (6-5)
First come roll	8	$25 and $30 odds (6-5)
Second come roll	4	$25 and $50 odds (2-1)
Next come roll	2	No effect on your bets
Next come roll	7	$50 win on your don't pass bet
		$100 win on both your don't come bets
		Total wins: $271
		Total losses: $37
		Net win $234

We keep increasing your bets during these series of cold rolls until the shooter finally makes his point. Then we start all over again, reverting to our basic 2 unit bet. Betting wrong with an aggressive strategy can be just as profitable as betting right.

Dice can remain "cold" for a long time as many right bettors know, and with a continual increase in your bets, you can take full advantage of a cold roll or series of rolls. However, should the shooter's luck turn, and he makes two points in a row, and you're quite a bit ahead, it would be time to leave the table as a winner.

12

Other Betting
Strategies

RECOMMENDED—WITH PLACE BETS ON THE 6 AND 8

This method is more daring and risky than the other bets because the house will be getting 1.52% on each of the place bets made. This strategy can be used with either single or double odds.

1. We bet 3 units on the pass-line with single odds or 2 units with double odds, and take our maximum free odds.

2. We now establish two come bets, at the same units bet as on our pass-line wager, with maximum free odds.

3. Here's the difference—if the 6 and/or 8 have not been covered by any of our previous pass-line and come bets, we bet 5 units on these numbers. Since each place betting unit is $6, our place bets will be $30 if we're betting in $5 units.

4. If these place bets repeat, we keep adding $12 or 2 $6 units to them each time they're rolled.

5. We always keep our two come bets working, and if a come bet is a 6 or 8, and the place bet has already been established, then

we take our place bet down, and leave our come bet with maximum odds.

For example, if your first two come bets were 5 and 9, and you had the 6 and 8 as place bets, and the 5 repeated, you would now make another come bet. If that come bet is a 6, you'd collect on your place bet of 6, take it down, and establish the come bet on 6 along with the free odds. Should this come bet on 6 repeat, then you'd make another come bet, meanwhile placing $30 on the 6 as a place bet.

6. The purpose of this strategy is not only to have two come bets working at all times, but also to have the 6 and 8 always covered—either as come bets or as place bets—in order to take advantage of a hot roll.

7. As our pass-line or come bets repeat, we increase them as in our basic aggressive strategy: with single odds we go from 3-5-6-9-12 and increase by 3 units from then on, and with double odds we increase by 2 units constantly from 2-4-6-8-10 and so on.

This is a more complicated system than our basic ones, but it allows us to always have the 6 and 8 covered, since they're the heart of any hot roll.

RECOMMENDED ONLY FOR THE DARING—ALL INSIDE NUMBERS COVERED AS PLACE BETS

This is the most risky of the recommended strategies, because its aim is to make the most money in the fastest possible time, giving the house a greater edge than it would have with the other methods of betting. It can be played with either single or double odds, but double odds are preferred.

1. We bet $15 on the pass-line, and take double odds on the point.

2. We make two come bets of $15 each, with double odds, establishing them.

3. We now cover all the inside numbers (5, 6, 8 and 9) that

haven't been covered by our previous bets. We'll be betting $25 on the 5 and 9 and $30 on the 6 and 8 as place numbers.

4. We only make our two come bets to establish the come numbers. Should any come bet repeat, that number will then be bet as a place number if it is an inside number. If it's a 4 or 10, the come number is simply taken down and no new come bet is made.

Thus, after our first two come bets are established, there will be no more made.

5. Every time a place number is rolled, we add 2 units to that number and its counterpart or twin. We'd thus add $10 each to the 5 and 9, and $12 each to the 6 and 8. If a 6 is repeated, for example, as a place number, we'd not only add $12 to it but to the 8 as well.

6. Should the point be made, we raise it by 3 units to 6 units or $30 and every time it repeats, we keep adding 3 units, always taking double odds.

7. Because of the prohibitive odds, we never cover the 4 and 10 as place numbers or buy them.

This method puts an awful lot of money on the layout and is recommended only for the most daring of players. It is useful, however, when a very hot roll is in progress, because you, as a winning player, can switch right into it from your basic strategy.

You may have increased your come bets considerably as numbers repeated, and yet not have had the 6 and 8 covered. You could then cover them with place bets. Or you might have all the inside numbers except the 5 covered by pass-line and come bets, and you might want to cover this number as well to get payoffs on every roll of the dice hitting inside numbers.

But it does give the house that 4% advantage on the 5 and 9, so I'd be extra cautious about playing it. It takes a lot of money but gives the most action—and the best win if a hot roll develops.

NOT RECOMMENDED—PASS-LINE AND ALL PLACE BETS COVERED

Most right bettors use the following system, which is not recommended at all because of the huge house advantage right from the start. And, with poor money management, it is a killer to any player.

1. Pass-line bet, with or without odds. Many of these players are superstitious and will only take odds on the outside numbers or on the 4 and 10, and if they do take odds on other numbers, they never take the maximum odds.

2. They then cover all the place numbers not covered by the pass-line bet. At this moment, they're giving the house an advantage up to 6.67% on the 4 and 10, as well as a constant 4% to the house on the 5 and 9.

3. If any number repeats, they immediately "press" or double it, instead of keeping most of the payoff by a gradual increase in betting units.

4. If a 7 shows on the dice right after the point is established, they lose every bet out on the layout at once—without collecting anything. By the time a hot roll comes along, 99% of these gamblers are out of chips and away from the table.

NOT RECOMMENDED—PASS-LINE AND OUTSIDE PLACE NUMBERS

1. A shocking number of craps players bet this way. They bet pass-line and only take odds if the number rolled is an outside point number—either 4, 5, 9 or 10.

2. Then they make place bets only on the outside numbers, giving the house the maximum edge on place numbers.

3. If any outside number should hit, they immediately press their bets. Usually, they never make a collection since it is rare for

two 4s to come up on any one roll. Some even press these bets up twice and then three 4s would have to appear for any kind of payoff to be made.

4. These players lose faster than the preceding group for they never collect on a 6 or 8 unless it's a pass-line point, and then they don't even take odds on the number.

NOT RECOMMENDED—PASS-LINE, ANY CRAPS AND ALL THE HARDWAYS

1. These bettors make a pass-line bet but, at the same time, to "protect this bet" they bet "Any Craps," thus giving the house an immediate 11.1%.

2. After the point is established, they usually save money for the Hardways by not betting on the free odds.

3. They bet all the Hardways, giving the house either 9.09% or 11.1% as its advantage.

4. Sometimes they bet place numbers, usually on the outside numbers or the 4 and 10 alone.

5. These bettors, if they have big credit with a casino, can run through $10,000 in a couple of hours, betting this insane way. And there are plenty of them at the tables.

Avoid the Not Recommended systems. Be careful about our most aggressive methods. Start conservatively—bet basic strategies with gradual increments as the roll develops. In this way, you'll not only be recognized as a "tough player" and one the casino fears, but you'll also be playing as astutely and intelligently as any craps player can. You'll be a winner.

13

A Dice Story

I first met Mr. L, and his wife, Fannie, in the coffee shop of the Frontier Hotel in Las Vegas one July weekend in 1977. Mr. L had some business dealings with a couple of gamblers I knew in Brooklyn and, when he told them he was going to do a little gambling in Las Vegas, they suggested that he look me up.

Mr. L was of indeterminate age, probably in his sixties. He was a short man of tremendous bulk, weighing close to 200 pounds, and had a large bald head. His wife was almost his twin, except that she had hair on her head of a bluish gray color of the type much favored by women of her age who frequent beauty parlors. Looking at them, I thought about the adage that people who are married long enough get to resemble each other. Mr. and Mrs. L certainly did. I was tempted to ask if they had a dog because dogs often resemble their masters, and I expected to see a fat hound wobble over to our table in the coffee shop, a cigar stuck in his mouth, breathing hard and puffing away. But there was no dog, only Mr. and Mrs. L.

I figured that our meeting would be brief. I would be polite and dutiful, say hello and good-bye, then go back to my work. But

Mr. L insisted that I join them for lunch, so I ordered a lox-and-cream-cheese plate.

"Eat, eat," he said, "it's all on the house. We're on a junket here."

"Have some extra tomatoes. It's better with tomatoes," said Fannie. I had the extra tomatoes and she ordered an extra bagel for me, as well as extra butter and cream cheese. Meanwhile both of them went to town, as dish after dish arrived, filled with calories.

Finally, stuffed, I sat back as they both studied the dessert menus. They examined the menus as if they were reading The Word, studying and discussing carefully all the possible choices. At last they had decided. Mrs. L was going to have cherry cheese cake and a side order of rice pudding, while Mr. L was limiting himself to three sweet rolls, all with nuts, and all smothered with butter. I opted for Jello, without the whipped cream.

"Put on whipped cream," Mrs. L informed the waitress. "This boy shouldn't eat Jello plain. It has no taste plain."

After dessert we sat back, because the Ls were unable to move for about fifteen minutes. Then they staggered to their feet and we went out of the coffee shop, freed at last from food.

"Now I'm going to do a little playing," he said.

"What do you play?"

"There's only one game," he said, "and that's dice. The other games, they're for the birds. Dice is action, and I came here for action."

"Well, enjoy yourself and good luck," I said, about to make my escape.

"No, no," said Mr. L, grabbing my arm. "Your friends told me you wrote books about games. You know all the odds . . . isn't that right?"

"Well, most of them."

"Watch me play. I want you to tell me what you think of my game."

"For a little while." I glanced at my watch. "Just for a little while."

"Perfect," said Mr. L.

"Perfect," repeated Fannie L. "I'm going to walk around and look around."

After his wife left, Mr. L relit a huge cigar that he had stuffed into his jacket pocket. "She doesn't like me to smoke in front of her. You know what my wife is going to do now?"

"No."

"She walks around by the slot machines and looks into all the . . . what do you call them, you know, where the money drops out when you win. She looks in there for nickels people might have left."

"Why does she do that?"

"Can you explain women? I can't. Come on." He took my arm firmly and we walked to the nearest craps table. Mr. L waved one fleshy hand to the dealer as we jammed into two available spaces.

"Sir?" asked the dealer.

"I want five hundred."

"Yes, sir." He looked over to the boxman, who turned his back and caught the attention of the floorman, who stared at Mr. L, then said to the dealer, "Give him the chips."

We got a stack of $5 red chips and a stack of $25 green ones. A new roll was about to begin. Mr. L put down two red chips on the pass-line. The roll was a 10.

"Love those tens," he told me, the cigar smoke swarming around our faces. He backed up his bet with $10 on odds, and then threw some chips on the table.

"Fifty-four dollars across the board," he said, and his chips were put in all the place boxes, $12 each on the 6 and 8, and $10 each on the 4, 5 and 9.

"Now comes the moment of truth," he said.

"You mean you don't want a seven?"

"Please, don't use that word. It's a dirty word."

The roll came down the table; a 7.

"Seven, line away," said the stickman, and all of Mr. L's chips were removed from the table. He had just lost $74 in thirty seconds. Meanwhile the floorman came over and Mr. L signed a marker for $500.

"New shooter coming out," yelled the stickman. "Bet those hardways, bet the field. Get those bets down. How about Any Craps, Craps Eleven?"

The players at the table rewarded this spiel with some chips thrown in the stickman's direction. Mr. L put $15 on the pass-line. The next roll was another 10.

"Now he rolls a ten. Now! Where was that ten when I needed it?" asked Mr. L. He grabbed some additional chips and bet $15 behind the line as an odds bet, and threw the dealer $54. "Across the board, my good man."

The shooter shook the dice and flung them to the far end of the table. Another 7.

"Seven, line away," said the stickman. Eighty-four dollars more down the drain.

"These dice are as cold as a witch's teat," said Mr. L, "and you know how cold that can be. But no matter, the worm has got to turn. Worms always turn, did you know that, my boy?"

I nodded and watched him put down $25 on the pass-line. The new shooter rolled a 6. Mr. L didn't take any odds. Instead he counted out $52 and gave it to the dealer.

"Across the board," he said. There was $2 less needed because the 6 wasn't a place number this time.

The next roll was a 9. Mr. L collected his $14. A few more numbers came up on the dice. Mr. L had collected $56 from his place bets.

"Now I'm even with them," he informed me, "and from now on it's all going to be gravy."

The next throw was a 7, however, and Mr. L was a net loser of $21 on the roll.

Within twenty minutes he lost his $500, took out another marker for $500, and lost that also, within the hour. I stayed around, not wanting to desert the sinking ship. When the one grand was gone, we left the table. Mr. L asked me to accompany him to the nearby lounge and he ordered a couple of Coors beers. He huffed and puffed and relit his cigar.

"Well, what do you think?" he asked.

"About what?"

"About my play. Did you ever see such cold dice? Ice cold. Popsicle dice."

"Well, you had a bad run."

"Yeah, what could I have done? I couldn't have done anything, could I? You have to admit, I couldn't have done anything but lose."

"You want my honest opinion?"

"Sure, why not? You know all about these games."

"You play a dumb game of craps."

The cigar nearly fell out of his mouth.

"What did you say?"

I repeated my statement, and he asked me why I felt that way.

"For one thing, you increase your bets when losing on the pass-line. And you only take odds when the point is 4 or 10. You're not taking advantage of free odds on any other point. You should back up each point with odds bets. And then you throw your money on the place numbers immediately. You're giving the house 6.67% on the 4 and 10. If you want to play them, at least buy them."

"What do you mean, buy them?"

"You can give the house a 5% commission and get 2 to 1 on the payoffs instead of 9 to 5."

"Is that what buy means?"

"Yes. And you never raise your bets. You had one good roll where you collected on about ten numbers, and you kept collecting your fourteen dollars and your eighteen dollars right up to the end of the roll. If you had raised your bets a little after each number repeated, you might have come out even from that one hot roll. The shooter made three or four points, all on sixes and eights and you didn't even have odds bets on them. Instead you fooled around with a bunch of hardway bets that never came through for you.

Actually, the table wasn't that cold . . . it was the way you handled
your bets that was terrible."

He drank his beer thoughtfully.

"Have you ever won at craps?" I asked him.

"Once . . . since I've been coming to Vegas. I caught a few hot
hands one weekend. I even held the dice for almost an hour once."

"How much did you win on that shoot?"

"About two thousand dollars."

"Holding the dice an hour?"

"Yeah . . ."

"You should have won $10,000."

"It's easy for you to say, win $10,000. You think you can do
better than I did?"

"I know I can."

"I'll tell you what," said Mr. L. "Let's be partners . . . you and
me."

I shrugged. I was anxious to get back to my writing, and I was
in no mood to gamble.

"I'll tell you what," he continued. "You take 25% of my action.
I'll play a thousand, and you have $250 of it, and if we win, you get
25% of the profits, and if we lose you lose 25% of whatever we
lose."

"Why should I do that? I can go over to the table now and bet
100% of my money and win or lose 100% of it. It's the same thing."

Just then Fannie came over, all excited. She had found a
couple of nickels on the floor near one of the slots. I took this
opportunity to say goodbye, but not before they extracted a
promise from me to have dinner with them that night.

That evening we ate at the Frontier Steak House, and the
meal took almost two and a half hours to complete. I tried to hold
back on the food, but it was practically impossible with these two
trenchermen. After the meal, during coffee, Mr. L had a proposition for me.

"You think you can beat the dice?" he asked.

"Sure, there's no guarantee, but it'll be much better than your method."

"I'll tell you what. I'm down about three big ones here, and this is my last night in Vegas. I'll go to the table with two thousand. Win, lose or draw, that's it. I'll either be out five grand or whatever . . . What part of the action do you want?"

"None, really."

"O.K. I'll give you this proposition. You get 25% of the winnings and 10% of the losings. What do you say?"

"On the two grand?"

"That's right. If we win, you get 25% of the profits, and if we lose, the most you can lose is $200. And we play your way. In fact, you can make all the bets."

I drank some coffee and thought about it, then said "O.K."

"Good, let's get the hell out of here and get some action."

When we got to the tables, I asked the dealer if they had single or double odds. The dealer said only single odds—they had discontinued double odds.

I took Mr. L aside. "Let's play at a casino with double odds."

"What difference does it make?"

"It can make a lot of difference. You said you were going to play my way, right?"

"Right."

"Double odds, then. Do you have credit anywhere else?"

"At the Dunes and the MGM."

"We'll go to the Dunes, then."

We left Fannie to look for her nickels and took a cab over to the Dunes. Mr. L signed a marker for two grand at the table. The floorman was happy to see him, and I could imagine the losses he had sustained at the Dunes. We were at a crowded table that was emptying out. Mr. L asked a player who was leaving how the action was.

"Cold, cold."

"Let's go to another table," Mr. L said.

"No. Let's play here. If we play at a hot table, the hot roll may already be over. Here it's cold. It's got to warm up."

He shrugged and looked at me quizzically, trying to figure out my last remark. We got two thousand in green $25 chips. Mr. L pushed them into the rails, and I picked up one green chip and put it on the pass-line.

"We'll test the waters," I said.

The first roll was a 3. A loser for us. Another $25 went on the pass-line. Another craps was rolled. One more loser.

I put another $25 on the pass-line. The point was 6. I laid $50 behind the line as a free odds bet. Then I put $25 out as a come bet. The next roll was a 7. We lost only the odds bet.

Mr. L had already been haranguing me about making place numbers. If we had bet his way, we would have lost all our bets instead of just the odds bet.

Again I made a pass-line bet, took double odds and made a come bet. Then another come bet, both with double odds. The shooter repeated the second come bet, but then sevened out. And so it went. We were really at a cold table. Our money was dwindling away. Slowly but surely it was evaporating, not helped by Mr. L's impulsive bet of $100 on all the place numbers on one roll, telling me that he had a "hunch." The shooter rolled a couple of 6s and then sevened out, and that was our biggest loss to date.

We were now down to $500. I told Mr. L to keep his hands off the chips, as the dice moved over to me. I was now the shooter. I put down $25 on the pass-line, not changing my pattern of betting. I rolled a 12.

"Another lousy shooter," the man next to me complained.

I put down another $25 on the pass-line. I rolled an 8. I put $50 behind the line as an odds bet, and made a $25 come bet. I immediately made the point the hard way. For once we started a roll winning money. I collected $85 for my winning pass-line bet, and threw $50 to the dealer as an odds bet on the come bet of 8. I rolled a 6 as my new point and put $100 behind the line, having raised my pass-line bet to $50. My money supply was fast disappearing. I took one of the few remaining $25 chips and placed it in the come box, and rolled a 9. Another $50 went on the odds. I shook the dice fiercely and threw them, as Mr. L yelled "Numbers, numbers."

I rolled a 9, and collected $100. I put $50 in the come box and rolled another 9. Now I put $100 on the free odds bet.

"Mr. L," I said, "I'm going all out. We have to recoup, and this roll is definitely heating up."

"I'm with you, my boy."

I bet $100 on the 5 as a place bet.

"Cover the 4 and 10," said Mr. L.

"No way. I don't want to give away too much to the house. We have all the inside numbers covered; they're the heart of a hot roll, and we'll go with them."

I shook the dice and threw them hard. A 6 came up. We collected $170 on the point, and I put $75 on the pass-line and rolled another 6, and put $150 on the free odds, and looked over the table. We had $25 bet on the 8 as a come bet with $50 odds; $50 on the 9 as a come bet with $100 odds, and $100 as a place bet on the 5.

"Numbers," screamed Mr. L.

And numbers showed on those dice. First I hit the 8, collected $85 and my come bet and replaced it with $120 as a place bet on that number. Then I rolled the 9, collected $200 on the come bet with odds and replaced it with $150 on the place bet of 9. I raised up the 5 to $150 also. Now we had the 5, 8 and 9 as place bets, and the 6 as a pass-line bet. The next roll was the 6 and we had $255 more in winnings.

I made the next pass-line bet $100. By this time the table was getting jammed, and chips were being bet left and right, as rumors of my hot hand spread through the casino. The dice were being flipped over by the stickman, over and over, before he returned them to me. The boxman was sweating and looking up at me with beady eyes. Beautiful. He was nervous. Even more beautiful.

I grabbed the dice and flung them.

"Yo-leven, winner," announced the stickman, as an 11 came up. The players were screaming with joy. I collected $100 and now bet $200 on the pass-line.

"Come on, seven," yelled a couple of players and 7 it was. Two hundred dollars more collected. I put down $300 on the pass-line.

Before the dice were returned to me, however, the boxman examined them. While he was doing this, I put a $25 chip on the pass-line and told the stickman this was for the boys, for the dealers.

When I got the dice back I shook them lightly and threw them across the table with a flick of the wrist. Seven again! I now raised the pass-line bet to $400, gave the dealers their $50 in winnings, and shook the dice. One more seven . . . but the point was a 4. I put $800 behind the line. I had made another $25 bet for the dealers and I backed that up with $25 odds.

I didn't like the 4 as a point, but there was nothing I could do but roll those dice and hope for the best, with $1,200 riding on the point. I was tempted to take off the $800 in free odds, but a small voice within me told me to stop thinking this way. Losers were defensive and fearful; losers made arbitrary odds bets and took them off on "hunches." The double odds bet on the 4 was correct— the house had no advantage on that bet and it reduced their edge. I put $150 on the place number 6 and shook the dice.

I threw the dice and rolled a 12, then a 3, 11, 2, 3 and another 12. I couldn't believe it. Not one collection in six rolls. I got back the dice and shook them fiercely, and flung them against the far end of the table. One die showed a 2 and the other was hidden behind a pile of chips. The dealer fished it out. It was a 2.

"Four, the hard way, winner on the pass-line," screamed the stickman. Not only had the dealers won $75 on my pass-line bet for them, but a whole bunch of players had made hardway bets for themselves and "the boys," and the dealers reaped a small fortune from that hard four.

I was even happier than the dealers. I collected $2,000 for the 4. My win on this bet was equal to the money we had started with at the table. It took a long time for all the bets to be paid off, and I waited patiently for the dice with Mr. L puffing away at a fresh cigar. He was all smiles.

I put $500 on the pass-line when the dice were returned to me. I flung them across the table, and now both were hidden among the masses of chips piled up as bets.

"Yo-leven," screamed the stickman, and the players screamed with him as an 11 showed on the dice. Everybody was a winner on that roll. Five hundred dollars more in yellow-and-black $100 chips were placed next to my bet.

I left $500 on the pass-line and waited for the dice. They were being examined by one of the boxmen. Another boxman had joined the table and the floormen were hovering around the table, all nervous. What greed there was at a casino! When the players won, how the casino personnel sweated! How distrustful they got! The casino wants to win all the time. But those dice belonged to me now, and there was nothing the boxman could do but return them to me. The magic cubes were now in my hands again. I smiled at the dice.

"Seven," Mr. L and the table yelled as I rolled them. They came up 2, a craps, a loser on the pass-line. A huge groan emanated from the players at the table.

"These dice are going to apologize," I said to Mr. L, and bet only $200 on the pass-line. I rolled a 10. Goddamn, I wasn't rolling inside numbers anymore. I placed $400 behind the line as a double free odds bet and then flung those cubes. A 2, 3, 11, 12 and 4 all appeared on the dice, without a single payoff for me.

I wanted numbers. I flung those dice again. Another 12. Now the boxman was smiling. He felt the dice were dying, that the roll was coming to an end. But Mr. L was more optimistic. He grabbed a handful of $100 chips off the rails.

"Make the 6 and 8,, $600 each and the 5 and 9 $500 each," he yelled to the dealer. He took another handful of chips. "I want to buy the 4 and 10," he said.

"No . . ."

"Please . . ."

"No!" I was now nervous about the big bets on the place numbers. We had $2,200 out on those numbers. I believe in orderly progressions, and lately the dice hadn't done anything but come up with craps.

Mr. L replaced the chips in the rails. "The worms are going to turn now," he said to me. He lit his cigar again, and I could see that his hands were shaking. Goddamn, we had a lot of money out on those place numbers.

I shook the dice. My heart was beating fast. I was finally swept up in this roll. I threw the dice, and rolled a 5. $700 collected quickly. Then a 9. $700 more. Then a 6 and another $700 came our way. Then two 8s worth $1,400.

The dice were taken and re-examined, not only by the boxmen, but by the pitboss himself. They looked them over and then looked me over. I stared back at them, and waited. It took a few minutes, but finally the dice were returned to me.

The next roll was a 6 and then a 9 and I followed this with another 6. Another $2,100 in profits. The table had come back to life, with everyone screaming, and people were standing three deep trying to see what was happening.

The dice were back in my hands. I shook them as before and threw them down to the other end of the table. One die spun around and came up a 3. The other showed a 4. I had finally sevened out.

I watched the dealers hurriedly grab all the chips that were on the layout and stack them up. Meanwhile our rails and pockets were stuffed with $25 and $100 chips.

Mr. L was on top of the world. "Let's really go to town, let's kill this casino," he said. He was ready to bet $500 on the pass-line with a new shooter coming out.

"No way. We got our hot roll. Now, let's get the hell out of here." Mr. L paid back his marker at the table, as the boxmen watched us sourly. I tipped the dealers a $100 chip, and we left the table, with Mr. L waddling alongside me. We cashed in our chips, and Mr. L gave me $1,200 for my hour's work at the tables. I thanked him and we went over to the lounge and had a couple of drinks to calm down. Then we took a cab back to the Frontier.

Fannie was waiting for us. She was hopping up and down.

Mr. L tried to pull out his wad of bills. "Honey . . ." he said, but she interrupted him.

"Look, look what I found. Look. I found it on the floor. Look." She was really hopping up and down.

In her hand was a shiny new dollar.

14

Junkets and Strategy for Junket Play

Many Nevada hotel-casinos, such as the major ones on the Las Vegas Strip, as well as giants like the MGM Grand in Reno, offer free junkets to those whom the casino executives term "qualified players." A qualified player is one who does a great deal of gambling and has a good credit rating.

The ideal junket member is a craps player who bets heavily and also has money or credit to back up his play. If he plays badly, the casino likes him even better because the house is counting on his big loss to offset the free services it offers to junket participants.

What is a junket? It is a trip organized for a group of qualified gamblers. They are all flown together to a hotel-casino, given free rooms, free food and liquor, and, sometimes, other free services. In addition to all this, the round-trip air fare is paid by the hotel and, in some instances, the wives or girlfriends are allowed to come along free, or if the gamblers are not really high rollers, they pay only for the woman's air fare. Once they are at the hotel, however, the women also get free room, food and liquor.

All this sounds like a good deal, but there's a rub to it. First of all, the casino expects each player to give the tables a certain amount of action. Generally speaking, the average play expected during a junket stay of four or five days is between $7,500 and $10,000. In the fancier and bigger hotels, more play is expected. In those hotels which are smaller or desperately need players, the action expected will be less.

How do you get on a junket? There are organizations which transport players to various Nevada hotels, and these clubs are located in most of the major Eastern and Midwestern cities. If you know of a player who goes on a junket and he can recommend you, that's the best way. If you know of an organization, that's good too. If you care to, you can write to the casino manager or credit manager of any major hotel in Nevada, asking about their junket program. Some have these programs, some do not. If they have a junket group regularly coming out from your area, the casino will advise you of the steps necessary to get involved.

These steps may include a check of your credit rating through bank accounts and your involvement as a gambler at other casinos. Sometimes the casino will take the word of another junket member if he says you're an "action player." They feel that one gambler knows another, and if the gambler that recommends you is a perennial and constant loser, it's even better. They'll welcome you with open arms.

Remember, most junket players are not only losers, but heavy losers—otherwise, there's no way the casino can afford to charter complete planes, pay the heads of junket organizations large fees, supply the players with free rooms, give them lavish meals and all the free liquor they can hold, and still turn a profit. And believe me, most of these junket programs are huge profit makers.

Suppose you follow our instructions and land on a junket. What then? You must realize that giving the house a play of $7,500 to $10,000 is giving them a great deal of action. That's fifteen or twenty trips to the craps tables, taking out markers of $500 each.

When you're on a junket, you don't play with cash. You

establish credit beforehand, and then you sign markers or IOUs against that credit. In this way, the casino knows exactly how much play you give them. And you must give them this action, or else they have the option of forcing you to pay the round-trip fare and billing you for all the services they've provided in terms of room, food and liquor.

Most of the casino personnel hovering around the craps table during your stay are floormen whose main job is to check, along with the boxmen and other casino employees, on just what kind of player you are. They watch all the members of the junket because the markers and total action don't reveal the whole picture. They know a player can go to a table, take out a marker for $500, make a couple of small bets, leave the table and cash in, and there goes $500 of so-called "action." With that kind of play, you can expect to get a bill for services rendered after one day, and you might be told to leave the hotel to make room for a real player.

Sometimes two players work out a method to avoid any real losses at the craps table. One will bet heavily on the pass-line and the other on don't pass. Those are the only bets they'll ever make and, in the end, neither loses much since they split any losses. They'll only lose when a 12 is rolled, in which case the pass-line player loses, and the don't pass bettor has a standoff. The casino has an edge of 1.40% on line bets and is content with it, but not from junket players playing this way.

If they find you working this scam, again you'll receive a bill for services rendered. I've spent many hours in casinos, not only as a professional player and writer, but also as the confidant of many high ranking casino personnel. I can tell you that most casinos today have elaborate methods of scrutinizing the junket players. These bettors are graded for *every session* they're at the tables, as to length of time there, kind of bets made, and patterns of play.

What kind of players do the casinos favor? Well, they love the foolish bettor with unlimited or high credit, the one who makes wild and improbable bets, who plays hunches, who sometimes backs up his line bets with odds and sometimes doesn't. They love the player who immediately covers all the place numbers and keeps pressing up his bets, betting heavy bucks on the hardways at the same time to "bring out" the numbers. They make a fortune from these kinds of players and there are plenty of them around.

But the casino will also tolerate a smart player—as long as he gives them action. Now, should you decide to go on a junket, try and pick a hotel that gives double odds if you're going to be a right or pass-line bettor. If you bet wrong, or don't pass, it doesn't really matter if you can lay single or double odds. Remember, you'll have to do the majority of your playing at the hotel where you stay because the casino expects your action. They didn't fly you out so you could play at a competitor's casino. But you're not expected to give them continual action, or to be at the tables all the time. All they want is the action you promised—legitimate use of the tables while you sign $7,500 or $10,000 worth of markers.

When selecting a hotel, the more fancy and spectacular the service and food, the more action you're expected to give. Perhaps you'll be content with a moderate establishment. I'm not suggesting any places in this book, but a few letters to various hotels in Nevada will give you the necessary information about hotel services and their minimum demands for action.

Let's suppose you pick a place where you have to play that $7,500. Remember, that's action, not losses. That's the total amount of markers you'll sign, not the money you'll be leaving at the tables. It's very possible that you'll come out a winner— especially after reading this book. Then what? The casino doesn't like the idea of you winning, of course, but that doesn't negate the free services or a return trip. In fact, they'll welcome you back for a chance to get their money on the next trip. The casino doesn't discriminate between winners and losers; what they want are players who will give them plenty of action.

If you study the basic winning strategies outlined in this book, you'll realize that betting pass-line with double free odds, then making two come bets with the same odds will give the house an expected edge of 0.6%. That's 60¢ for every $100 bet as their profit.

For every $1,000 worth of play you give the house they should win $6, theoretically.

A good run of the dice, with steady increases in the size of your bets may very well win you a great deal of money at several of those mandatory sessions at the tables, more than enough to compensate for the house edge. This is not to say that you'll automatically lose $6 for each $1,000 of play, but in the long run that's what you should lose.

As I've said, before you get to the casino, you should know what minimum bet is expected of you at the craps tables. It might be $10, $15 or $25 or more. If the minimum bet is rather large, you have to decide whether you have enough capital to warrant this kind of enforced action. If you're comfortable making only $5 bets, don't get involved in a junket. If you do, you'll be sweating out every session of play with scared money, and the anxiety will ruin your trip.

But, if you can find a comfortable betting limit, have the money to back it up, and have the controls to play tough—as suggested in this book—it might be well worth a try. You'll be out in the sunshine and the open spaces of Nevada; you can enjoy the swimming pools, tennis courts and golf courses as well as the fine food and room service. It's very possible, with the knowledge you now have, that you'll come home with not only pleasant memories, but with the casino's money as well.

15

Craps as a Private Game

INTRODUCTION

Because craps has been played for well over two thousand years, there are many versions of the game practiced throughout the world.

Long before casinos came into existence, craps was played as a private game—and it is often played that way still. It is played in homes as well as in the alleys and the streets of towns and cities all over America. Craps is a very popular gambling game because it is a great money game requiring minimal equipment—two dice and cash, of course, and other gamblers. There is no elaborate layout and no dealers, boxmen, or floormen need to be around.

As you might have guessed, the casino game is an offshoot of the private game. Since the casino books all bets at the craps table, a layout is necessary to show all bets, and dealers have to be employed to keep track of these bets. The original craps layouts

were simple matters. As time went on, they became more and
more complex, as casinos added bets to assure action on every roll
for the benefit of the house, not the player.

The more bets allowed, the more the casino profited. It
arranged a craps layout where every bet was to the player's
disadvantage, with the exception of the free odds bet. Probably the
free odds bet is only allowed as a nod to the private game, where it
is an integral part of the action. Players would protest when it was
not permitted; yet the casinos are very shy about advertising that
bet, and it never shows on the casino craps layout.

With dealers working the game, it is possible to have and keep
track of continuous betting on the come and don't come boxes, as
well as hardway bets and all the involved proposition bets.

Most of the center proposition bets are never used in private
games. Certainly there are no Field Bets, no place bets and rarely
are there come bets. The private game is simplicity itself and its
popularity has always remained high. Whenever men gathered on
the street outside a factory on pay day, or when soldiers were paid
on the first of the month, if someone had a pair of dice, a game
could be gotten up in a matter of minutes.

In this section, I'm dealing solely with the private game. It is
different not only from the casino game as played in Nevada and
Atlantic City, but from any illegitimate or semi-legal game played
in private clubs where any form of layout is used, where the dealers
work for the house, and where the casino books all bets. In a
private game, every player has a chance to roll the dice and to book
all his own bets. Players bet with each other, not against the house;
thus there is no house edge to buck. In the private game, everyone
is on his or her own.

THE BASIC GAME OF PRIVATE CRAPS

The game can be played with at least two players and as many
as want to participate because side bets are allowed among players.

The average game attracts anywhere from four to ten players. Each bettor has a turn at rolling the dice, and some kind of order or arrangement is usually established so that everyone can be a shooter. Any player may refuse to roll the dice when it is his or her turn.

The same basic game as in casino craps is played involving a come-out roll with players betting with or against the dice, and giving or taking odds on every point. However, there is one slight difference in the private basic game, and that involves the 12. This will be explained in the following rules of play.

1. The shooter, and any other players who care to, may bet with the dice, betting that the dice will pass, or win. They are the right bettors. On the come-out roll, if the shooter rolls a 7 or 11, all the right bettors immediately win their bets, and the wrong bettors lose theirs. If a 2, 3 or 12 is rolled, all the right bettors immediately lose their bets, and all the wrong bettors win. There is no standoff on either the 12 or 2, as in casino craps. This gives the wrong bettor a slight advantage over the right bettor of approximately 1.4%.

2. If any other number is rolled on the come-out roll (4, 5, 6, 8, 9 or 10) it becomes the point and must be repeated before a 7 is rolled for the right bettors to win. If a 7 comes up before the point is repeated, then the right bettors lose and the wrong bettors win.

3. After any point is established, the players may bet with the point or against it by making odds bets. Any player may make an odds bet, either laying or taking odds, whether or not he has bet on the roll previously. For example, a player may have avoided making any bets until the point was established. If the point is 5, he may now lay 3-2 against it, or take 3-2 by betting with the shooter.

4. The odds bets are generally, but not always, true odds. They are always true on the 4, 5, 9 and 10, but many times in private games players lay even-money against the 6 and 8, when the true odds are 6-5. When a right bettor takes even-money on these points, he is giving the wrong bettor a 9.09% advantage on the bet.

Even-money bets are made on these numbers (6 and 8)

through ignorance of the odds or through laziness. Many players know that the odds are really 6-5, but feel that an even-money bet doesn't really make that much difference in the long run, not realizing that 9.09% is a terrific disadvantage.

As in casino craps, the odds on the 5 and 9 are 3-2 against the point being made, and it's 2-1 against the 4 and 10.

Here's how the game is usually played:

A shooter is selected, and he picks up the dice and prepares to throw them against a wall or other backboard so that they'll have a random bounce. He now puts down cash in front of him, and asks who'll "fade" or cover his bet, sometimes called a "center bet."

Let's assume he puts down $10 as his bet. Players may cover all or part of this bet. A player may say "I've got $2," or "I've got $5 of it," or "I've got it all." Money is thrown down in separate piles next to the $10 until it is fully covered. These players are betting against the dice by fading the shooter.

At the same time, other players may bet with or against the dice. A player may say "I'm with the shooter," and lay down $20. All or part of this may be covered by other bettors. Whatever amount isn't covered, the player picks up and returns to his pocket.

Other players announce that they're betting against the shooter, and they can put down their money to be faded. If the bettor wants to put down more than the original shooter, he may. There are no limits as long as some other gambler is willing to fade the bet.

After all the bets are down, the shooter rolls the dice. Let's assume his come-out roll is a 10. At this point, the shooter or other players betting with the dice may announce that they're interested in taking odds on the 10. Other players may state that they're laying 2-1 against the 10. More bets are made.

Now the shooter picks up the dice again and continues his roll. All that interests the players is whether or not he makes that point. If a 10 repeats before a 7 shows, all the right bettors collect their winning bets. If the 7 shows first, then the wrong bettors win, and pick up their winning bets.

Very rarely are other kinds of bets made, though any type can be made if the person offering the bet finds a taker. A player may say "I give 30 to 1 against a 12 showing on the next roll," and he might find takers. Another player will ask if he can get 17-1 that an 11 shows on the next roll. He may or may not get takers for his bet. But, these side bets are rarities. The big money in private games is bet on the come-out roll and on the point as an odds bet.

The player I've described in this chapter is a $10 bettor, but there are private games that can run into the thousands of dollars, all in cash payments.

In the casino game, especially in the major casinos, the assumption is that the game is on the level and the dice used are legitimate and not crooked ones. There is no such assumption to be made in a private game. Usually one of the players digs out a pair of dice from his pocket. The dice are smaller than ordinary casino dice, and often have rounded edges, more often beaten up and nicked. There is no way you can tell if they're legitimate dice. And if you play for money, you want at least an honest set of dice.

I've been involved in private games where I knew several of the players to be honest men, but still there was no way I could be certain the dice were on the level. If the throws seem random enough, that is one safeguard. Of course, dice can be switched for specific rolls, and if enough money is involved, crooks can also get into the action.

This is not to say you should be paranoid about private games, but be alert and wary—especially if you're betting big money.

Private craps games have their own style and language. In the casino game, whenever a 2 or 12 is rolled, the stickman will simply announce, "Two, a craps," or "Twelve, a craps," but there are more flamboyant names for these numbers in the private game. A 2 is "snake eyes," and a 12 is "boxcars." A 4 is "little Joe," or "little Joe from Kokomo." When an 8 is the point, the right players are shouting for an "Eighter from Decatur."

If the point is a 10, players will be calling for the "Big Dick," to repeat. "Fever" is often used for a 5. Other terms are "Ninety

Days" for a 9, and "Jimmy Sticks" for a 6. There are many other expressions, depending on the region and the players involved.

To summarize the private game of craps:

1. All players have the right to shoot the dice, and they are selected in some kind of order. A player may refuse to be a shooter, however. When the shooter makes a bet, he is betting that the dice will win, or pass, and those players who bet against the dice are called "faders" because they "fade" or cover the shooter's bet.

2. Players may bet among themselves, either on the come-out roll, or after a point is established. On the come-out roll, players may bet with or against the dice, if they can find other players to fade their bets.

3. On the come-out roll, the same rules apply as in casino craps, with two exceptions. A 7 or 11 is an immediate winner for the right bettors, and an immediate loser for the wrong ones. A 2, 3 or 12 is an immediate loser for the right bettors and an immediate winner for the wrong bettors. There is no standoff on the 2 or 12 as there is in casino craps.

4. After a point is established, the shooter and other players may take or lay odds on the point. Any player may make an odds bet even if he hasn't bet on the come-out roll. Sometimes a 6 or 8 is bet at even-money instead of the correct 6-5, but generally, all point bets are wagered at the correct odds.

5. If the point is made (repeated) the right bettors win. If a 7 is rolled before the point is made, the wrong bettors win.

6. Sometimes other bets are made—and any kind of bet is permitted—if a gambler can find a taker for his bet.

16

A Winning Strategy for Private Games

When playing in a private game, your initial attitude should be one of caution, and you should be in no hurry to get your bets down. Stand around for awhile and watch the way the dice bounce. Make sure that they are rolled against some kind of firm backboard. Don't play where only a blanket is spread on a floor and the dice are rolled without striking any barrier. There are cheats who can "pinch" the dice and control the numbers coming up on "blanket rolls."

If you can, pick up the dice and examine them so that you'll recognize other spurious dice introduced into the game. If you feel secure and believe that the game is on the level, then make your first bet; but, if you have any doubts about its honesty, forget about action. Don't be a sucker.

In the private game, the wrong player has an advantage over the right bettor, because the 12 is not barred as a winning bet to those who bet against the dice. If you want to take advantage of this small edge, always bet wrong on the come-out roll.

On any point established, if you lay odds, you will not give the right bettors any advantage at all, and if you can lay even-money on the 6 and 8, you'll have a big edge with which to work. I was involved in a weekly poker game a few years back, where I was a constant winner. I won because I was the best player in that particular game, and since poker is a game of skill, my skill prevailed. After a while the other players grew restless. Because they thought poker was a game of luck, they never barred me from their game. They were always waiting for their bad luck to end and for my good luck to vanish; but since luck wasn't involved, these unlikely events never transpired.

After a year of losses, they began playing craps after every session of poker, trying to win their money back that way. The host would produce a pair of dice, we'd clear an area of furniture and roll against the nearest wall. I bet wrong on the come-out and rarely ever shot the dice. When I did roll, I bet only a small amount as my center bet and took the odds if a point was established.

When I wasn't the shooter, I'd always try to cover the shooter's center bet, giving myself that 1.4% edge. If a point was other than the 6 and 8, I'd rarely give odds, but if it was a 6 or 8, I was allowed to lay even-money against the point. Occasionally, a shooter would get on a fantastic roll and beat me for the evening, but my 1.4% edge on the come-out roll and my 9.09% advantage on the 6 and 8 points eventually prevailed. After I took their money in poker, I cleaned them out in craps.

And that's my advice to you. Bet wrong and if you can lay even-money on the 6 and 8, pour it in. If you must give 6-5, which are the correct odds, you can either lay the odds or not. It doesn't really matter because it's an absolutely even bet, and the right player will have no advantage on the bet. You'll then have to be satisfied with your 1.4% edge—and if the casinos are happy about this advantage, you should be too.

Of course, if you really want to gamble, you can do so with impunity in an honest private game because, at worst, with single odds, betting right, you're giving the wrong bettor only 0.8% on your wagers, and if you bet wrong and lay odds, you have the edge.

But, above all, be certain that the game is on the level. With this advice, I don't see how you can lose. If you seek out honest games, eventually you'll find one where 6s and 8s are bet against at even-money, and that's your chance to pick up some quick cash.

17

Cheating at Dice

Any game that depends upon the result of two plastic cubes thrown across a floor or table is prey to crooks and when a great deal of money is at stake, the cheats swarm like sharks. If there is cheating going on in casinos, it is generally the casinos that are being cheated, rather than the players. I'm referring now to established major casinos in Nevada and Atlantic City.

Crooked or tampered dice are legal evidence and no major casino would take the chance of jeopardizing its license—which might be worth millions of dollars—in order to fleece a table of gamblers out of a few thousand bucks. If you study the profits of the major casinos, the average net profit on each craps table they operate is over a million dollars a year in Las Vegas (and it seems much higher than that in Atlantic City). Why should a casino bother to gyp a few thousand out of unsuspecting players, when they can win it legally, by just running a game?

The cheating that does occur in casinos is generally conducted by players who might work as a team. For example, one man would bet huge amounts of money on the layout just prior to the switch of crooked or loaded dice by another player in the game. This way it doesn't appear that the two players are connected in any way.

If a player can get phony dice into a game—dice that won't come up 7, for instance—and they are introduced right after a point has been established, the team can make a small fortune with a limited number of rolls, by betting the place numbers to the limit. With five rolls they can pull down close to $4,000. They can then pull the crooked dice out of the game and have the regular roll resume.

The casino fears such crooks and takes all kinds of precautions against this happening. For one thing, the dice put into the game at the outset of play, when a table is opened, are made specifically for the casino, with its logo and name printed on the dice. In addition, most casinos have their dice numbered, and these numbers are continually checked by the boxman whenever a die flies off the table or if there is a hot roll in progress.

The stickman also helps prevent cheating by constantly turning over the dice with his stick to make sure that each die has the requisite six numbers on it. If a die was made up of even numbers only (as some crooked dice are) then it would be impossible for a 7 to appear. The roll could go on forever, with 4s, 6s, 8s and 10s continually showing, and the place bettors would clean up.

Therefore, the casino is ever alert to switched dice and to the possibility that a dealer might work in collusion with a cheat to allow switched dice into a game without reporting them.

In addition to the boxmen and the dealers, the floormen also watch the table's action and look for anything strange or unusual happening. When there is some commotion at one end of the table—a fainting spell, a spilled drink, or any kind of upset, they become very alert. While attention is directed to the disrupted area, it is the duty of one of the boxmen and the floormen to look to the other end of the table to see just what's going on there.

Some teams not only work to cheat the house, but the players as well. They're not interested in crooked dice, but in the player's chips which are jammed into the rails. These chips aren't securely in place and only the player's body acts as a shield between the chips and a potential thief. The "rail thieves" usually concentrate on the shooter, who has his eye on the table, not on his chips. At the same time, his body is thrust forward in the act of shooting, and there are moments when his chips are unguarded, especially during a crowded and hectic game. As the shooter bends forward to throw the dice, the thief does likewise, and as all eyes are on the dice, he moves stealthily and quickly to remove chips from the shooter's rails.

I know this has been done, and is still being done in casinos. I've interviewed these thieves, who call themselves "crossroaders," and they've shown me how they operate—but not under actual casino conditions. They have a lot of good moves, so my advice to players is to protect themselves from rail thieves, including other players. Occasionally, other gamblers at the table, losing and desperate, may take a chance by stealing chips from their neighbors at the table.

As I've mentioned earlier, over every craps table in the Nevada casinos is a one-way mirror, called "the eye in the sky." From this vantage point, a casino employee can watch the action at a table below and spot any cheating. Generally, these observers are watching the dealers and other casino personnel, making sure that they don't steal or remove casino chips from the table. They can also spot cheats switching dice or stealing other players' chips. However, the eye in the sky is not always in operation over each table because there are usually only one or two men up there watching the operations of an entire casino, and it is impossible for them to watch every move at every table.

If you play for serious money, gamble in the major casinos. You can be sure the casino is not trying to cheat you. Watch out for sudden moves at the table, upsets and commotions. When they happen, protect your chips. Always keep an eye on your chips, making certain that you stand so that you're protecting them. If you're winning heavily, cash in some chips for larger denomination chips, and place them in an inner pocket.

PRIVATE GAMES AND PRIVATE CASINOS

When playing in illegitimate private casinos, you must be wary, not only of other players and thieves among the spectators, but of the casino itself and its equipment. They have no valuable license to protect—all they have to do is pay off the local authorities to run their game. Often, these casinos are linked to the underworld and organized crime feels that all bettors and gamblers are fair game to be cheated, ruined and destroyed.

Be careful in any illegal game. If possible, avoid them, but if you find yourself at one of these establishments, bet moderately and carefully. See which way the trend is going. Some friends of mine invited me to one of these private casinos in a city that shall remain nameless. I was at a table where every player was betting with the dice, betting right. Not one point was made in the first half hour I at the table. I had made a few $5 bets on the pass-line, then quickly switched to bigger bets on don't pass. If there was cheating going on, at least I was going with the house—and against the grain, as it were—and in the process making good money. After all, in an illegal game, what can a player do? Complain about the dice? Call in the police? If they're being paid off, and you can be certain they are every time an illegal game is in operation, whose side will they be on? So, I simply went with the house, won a small bundle, and got the hell out of the casino just as soon as my poor friends were cleaned out.

They were amazed that I had won, and told me the game was on the level. How would they know? I'm a realist, not a moralist. If an illegal game is going on, I'm not going to blow the whistle, but that doesn't mean that I have to believe that it's on the up and up. In an illegal casino, there's no reason for anything to be legal.

There's no law in these places but the law of money, and the first rule of that law is greed.

In private games, run either by individuals or as spontaneous games, such as those taking place in an alley or doorway, be extra careful of the dice and the players. Here, no layout is used, but individual bets are made among the players themselves. If you lust for action and flash a bunch of bucks, a whole gang of cheats may arrange a game just to wipe you out. Be careful. I can't keep repeating words like careful, caution, wary, often enough. Keep your eyes and ears open. After all, it's your money.

In some of these games, crooked dice don't even have to be switched into the game. They're the standard dice already in use. And even if legitimate dice are in the game, there are players I've heard of who can roll just about any number they care to if there's no backboard for the dice to bounce off. And other shooters can literally "run the scales," that is, they can start with the 2 and roll consecutive numbers right up to the 12. What chance are you going to have against them?

This is not to say that these games are always crooked. I'm not asking you to become paranoid or to accuse everyone involved in these games of being a cheat. What I'm suggesting is that they *might not* be on the level, and if you lose, there's nothing you can do about it, and there's no one you can complain to. It's better to be careful in the first place. Try not to be a loser but above all, don't be a sucker.

CROOKED DICE

This book is not a primer on cheating, but here are some things that can be done to dice to make them illegal or crooked.

1. Dice may be shaved or sanded down so that certain numbers appear more often than others, either as passing or missing dice. These are also called percentage dice.

2. Dice may be hollowed out and then weighted with slugs or

other material so that certain sides will fall flat more often than others, giving a higher percentage of rolls favoring certain numbers. These are known as loaded dice.

3. Dice, called "Tops and Bottoms," have certain numbers missing, either all the even or all the odd numbers, so that these dice may come up with numbers other than 7s, or with many 7s and 11s. Sometimes one die has only even numbers and the other odd numbers. In that case it's practically impossible to repeat certain points.

DICE CHEATS

1. Dice can be held in the cheat's hand so that it appears they are shaking within his grasp, but all they do is make a rattling noise, and when they are thrown, they are forced out just the way the cheat wants them to roll.

2. A blanket roll makes use of no backboard, and the dice are controlled to rest on a certain number after being "pinched" or held in a certain way.

3. Backboard rolls are thrown directly against a soft backboard, which deadens the spin, allowing the dice to fall on a predetermined number.

4. A good cheat can switch a pair of crooked dice into his hands in a flash, faster than the eye can see.

Although there are tests for crooked dice, such as water tests for loaded dice, the best defense is to play with transparent dice, and to have a hard-surfaced backboard to roll the dice against. But these are only stopgap measures against a determined cheat. The best protection is to play among people you know and trust and, if possible, in a licensed casino where, although the odds may be slightly against you, at least you know you've got an honest game.

Glossary

ACE   The one spot on a die.

ADVANTAGE   See *House Advantage*.

ANY CRAPS   A one-roll bet that the next throw of the dice will be a craps, a 2, 3 or 12.

ANY SEVEN   A one-roll wager that the next throw of the dice will be a 7.

BACKBOARD   Some form of barrier in a private craps game to assure that the dice will have a random bounce.

BACK LINE WAGER   A bet, laying odds, on the don't pass or don't come.

BANK CRAPS   Another term for the game of casino craps, since the casino books all bets.

BAR THE 12   Shown on the craps layout in Las Vegas to ensure that the casino has an advantage over the wrong bettor.

BASE   See *On Base*.

BEHIND THE LINE   A wager on the free odds after a point has been established on the come-out roll.

BETTING RIGHT   Betting that the dice will pass; with the dice.

BETTING WRONG   Wagering against the dice; that they won't pass.

BIG DICK   A slang expression for the 10.

BIG 6 AND BIG 8   A wager at even-money that the 6 or 8 will repeat before a 7 is rolled.

BLANKET ROLL   A roll by a cheat who controls the dice while rolling on a surface without any backboard.

BOXCARS   A slang term for the roll of 12.

BOXMAN   A casino employee who supervises the game of craps, and remains seated during the play.

BRING OUT   A term used by dealers and players when betting on the hardway of the point, to "bring out" the point, i.e., to make it come out on a roll of the dice.

BUY THE 4 OR 10   To pay a 5% commission to the casino in order to be paid the correct odds of 2-1 on the place numbers 4 and 10.

CASINO ADVANTAGE   See *House Advantage*.

CASINO CHECKS   The casino's term for chips used during play.

CENTER BET   In private craps, the term for the shooter's bet on the come-out roll.

CHANGE COLOR   To change chips into lower or higher denominations.

CHEAT   A crook who introduces phoney dice or tampers with legal dice at a craps game.

CHIPS   The common term for tokens, issued by a casino in place of money, and having the equivalent of cash.

COLD DICE   Dice which consistently don't pass.

COME BET   A bet with the dice that they will pass, made after the come-out roll.

COME BOX   The area on the layout where a come bet is made.

COME-OUT ROLL   The initial or first roll of the dice before a point has been established.

CRAPS   The term for a roll of 2, 3 or 12.

CRAPS OUT   To throw a craps on the come-out roll.

CREW   Four dealers who staff a craps table at a casino.

CROOKED DICE   Dice that have been tampered with so as not to give a random roll.

CROSSROADER   A crook who will cheat at any type of casino game.

DEALER   A casino employee who helps operate a craps game.

DICE   A pair of cubes, each with six sides and each numbered from 1 to 6, whose combinations, when rolled, determine payoffs and losses in the game of craps.

DIE   A single cube, singular of dice.

DON'T COME BET   A bet made after the come-out roll, that the dice will not pass.

DON'T COME BOX   The area on the layout where a don't come bet is made.

DON'T PASS BET   A bet made on the come-out roll that the dice will not pass.

DON'T PASS LINE   The area on a layout where a don't pass bet is made.

DOUBLE ODDS BET   A free odds bet made at double the amount of the original bet.

EASY, EASY WAY   The roll of a 4, 6, 8 or 10 where the dice are not matched as a pair, such as 2-2, but in other combinations.

EDGE   The advantage either a player or casino has on a particular wager. Usually described as a percentage (%).

EIGHTER FROM DECATUR   A slang term for the 8 in private craps.

EVEN-MONEY   A payoff at 1-1.

FADE   To cover a shooter's bet in a private game of craps.

FADER   One who covers a shooter's bet or part of it, in a private game of craps.

FIELD BET   A bet that the next roll of the dice will come up 2, 3, 4, 9, 10, 11 or 12.

FIELD NUMBER   One of the numbers in a Field Bet.

FLOORMAN   A casino employee who stands behind the craps table, checking on the players and authorizing credit for players.

FREE ODDS   Another term for any odds bet where the house has no advantage.

HARDWAY BET   A wager that the dice will come up as an even pair on either a 4, 6, 8 or 10 before they come up easy or a 7 is rolled.

HARDWAYS   The term for the 2-2, 3-3, 4-4 and 5-5.

HIGH ROLLER   A bettor who wages large sums of money at a craps table.

HOP BET   A one-roll wager on a number not in the center layout.

HORN BET   A one-roll wager on the 2, 3, 11 and 12.

HOT HAND   A shooter who has dice that are continually winning is said to have a "hot hand."

HOT ROLL   Dice that are continually passing, and that are held by a shooter for a long time before sevening out.

HOUSE ADVANTAGE   The edge a casino has over a player on a particular bet on the craps layout.

INSIDE NUMBERS   The numbers 5, 6, 8 and 9. Usually designated as inside numbers when being bet as place numbers.

JIMMY STICKS   A slang term in private craps for the 6.

JUNKET   An organized group of gamblers who are treated to free air-fare, room, food and liquor in return for their play and action at the casino which sponsors them.

LAYOUT, CRAPS LAYOUT   An imprint on a felt surface showing all the bets that can be made in a casino, with spaces for those bets.

LAY THE ODDS   An odds bet by a wrong bettor against a number, giving odds.

LAY WAGER   A place bet by a wrong bettor, who pays a 5% commission for making such a bet.

LIMIT, BETTING LIMIT   The maximum bet that the casino will accept on its layout, or on any individual bet.

LINE BET   Another term for a pass-line and don't pass bet.

LITTLE JOE, LITTLE JOE FROM KOKOMO   A slang term for the 4.

LOADED DICE   Dice that have been weighted to tamper with their roll.

MISS, MISS-OUT   A term for a roll where a shooter sevens out.

NATURAL   Another term for a 7 or 11 rolled on the come-out roll.

NICKELS   Insider's term for $5 chips at a casino.

NUMBERS   The call of right bettors for the 4, 5, 6, 8, 9 or 10 to appear on the dice.

ODDS   The correct ratio determining whether or not an event will occur at a craps table.

ODDS BET   See *Free Odds*.

OFF   An oral call by a player that his bet will not be working on the next roll of dice. Also, a term signifying that certain bets are not working, e.g., place numbers on a come-out roll.

ON BASE   The term for a standing dealer who is not the stickman.

ONE-ROLL BETS   A wager whose outcome is determined by the next throw of the dice.

ON THE STICK   The term to signify that a dealer is now working the stick, and is the stickman for a designated time.

OUTSIDE NUMBERS   The 4, 5, 9 and 10.

PASS   A winning decision for the dice.

PASSING, DICE ARE PASSING   A term to signify that the dice are coming up winners for the pass-line bettors.

PASS-LINE   The area on the layout where a pass-line bet is made.

PASS-LINE BET   A wager that the dice will win, or pass.

PAYOFF   The collection of a winning bet.

PERCENTAGE DICE   A term for certain crooked dice which favor the cheat over the long run.

PITBOSS   A casino employee in charge of all the craps tables in one area of the casino, known as the craps pit.

PLACE NUMBERS, PLACE BETS   A wager on the numbers 4, 5, 6, 8, 9 and 10 in the place number or place box area of the layout.

PLAYER   Another term for gambler or bettor.

POINT   The number 4, 5, 6, 8, 9 or 10 when rolled on the come-out roll.

PREMIUM PLAYER   The casino term for a high roller.

PRESS, PRESS A BET   To increase a bet, usually by doubling.

PROPOSITION BETS   The bets in the center layout.

QUALIFIED PLAYERS   Players who meet the casino's credit standards for junkets.

QUARTERS   An insider's term for $25 chips.

RAILS   A grooved area at the craps table where players place their chips when they aren't being bet.

RAIL THIEF   A crook who steals chips from the players' rails.

RIGHT BETTOR   A player who bets that the dice will pass or win.

ROLL   A single throw of the dice. Also, a complete series of throws until the shooter sevens out.

ROLLER   See *Shooter*.

SEVEN OUT   To throw a 7 after a point has been established, ending the roll, and losing with the dice.

SHOOT   A term for the complete series of rolls before a seven-out.

SHOOTER   The player who rolls or throws the dice, and whose throws determine all payoffs and losses at the table or in a private game.

SNAKE EYES   A slang term for the number 2.

STANDOFF   A situation where no decision results from a throw of the dice on certain bets.

STICKMAN   The dealer who calls the game and handles the stick at a casino craps game.

SWITCH DICE   To secretly exchange one set of dice for another, crooked set.

TAKE THE ODDS   To make an odds bet as a right bettor, thus getting better than even-money on a winning bet.

TIP   See *Toke*

TOKE   A gratuity given to a dealer by a player.

TOPS AND BOTTOMS   Crooked dice which only have three numbers on each cube or die.

WITH THE DICE, BETTING WITH THE DICE   Wagering that the dice will win, or pass.

WORKING   A signification that bets are on, and payoffs will be made on the next roll of the dice. For example, the don't come bets are working on the come-out roll.

WRONG BETTING   Betting against the dice by betting don't pass or don't come.

WRONG BETTOR   A player who bets don't pass, betting against the dice.

YO-LEVEN   A slang term used by stickmen to signify the number 1'

Index